Reform and Development in Deng's China

Edited by
Shao-chuan Leng

Volume IV
The Miller Center Series
on Asian Political Leadership

UNIVERSITY
PRESS OF
AMERICA

Lanham • New York • London

The Miller Center

University of Virginia

Co-published by arrangement with
The Miller Center of Public Affairs,
University of Virginia

The views expressed by the author(s) of this publication do not necessarily
represent the opinions of the Miller Center. We hold to Jefferson's dictum that:
"Truth is the proper and sufficient antagonist to error, and has nothing to
fear from the conflict, unless by human interposition, disarmed of her
natural weapons, free argument and debate."

Library of Congress Cataloging-in-Publication Data

Reform and development in Deng's China / edited by
Shao-chuan Leng.
p.   cm. — (The Miller Center series on Asian
political leadership ; v. 4)
Revised papers presented at a conference on "Reform and
Development in Deng's China", held at University of
Virginia in November 1992.
Includes index.
1. China—History—1976–   —Congresses.   2. Teng, Hsiao-p' ing
1904–   —Congresses.   I. Leng, Shao Chuan.   II. Series.
DS779.2.R44   1994   951.05—dc20   94–4725 CIP

ISBN 0–8191–9503–0 (cloth : alk. paper)
ISBN 0–8191–9504–9 (pbk. : alk. paper)

The paper used in this publication meets the minimum requirements of
American National Standard for Information Sciences—Permanence
of Paper for Printed Library Materials, ANSI Z39.48–1984.

Dedicated to

Nora and David

Table of Contents

Preface

KENNETH W. THOMPSON
Director, the Miller Center of Public Affairs

The present volume is the fourth in a series on Asian political leadership. Volume I examined *Changes in China: Party, State, and Society*. It has been highly praised for its important contribution to an understanding of change in China. By focusing on the party, state, and society, the volume is an important addition to our understanding of social and political life in China. The second volume has gained recognition from several national associations that choose the best books in various fields. It was cited as one of the most outstanding books of 1990. Entitled *Coping with Crises: How Governments Deal with Emergencies*, it employs the comparative method in analyzing emergencies in nation-states in far-flung corners of the world. It represents a pioneering study of the success and failure of governments in dealing with crises. The third volume constitutes a study of *Chiang Ching-Kuo's Leadership in the Development of the Republic of China on Taiwan*. It brings together writings by the best-informed observers, diplomats, and scholars with backgrounds on China on Taiwan.

The fourth volume is *Reform and Development in Deng's China*. It looks back on reforms affecting China's economy and people and ahead to the future. In his introduction, Professor S.C. Leng addresses a series of questions, the answers to which will determine China's future. Contributors such as Leng, Doak Barnett, Robert Scalapino, John Fei, Jack Hou, Robert Sutter, and Deborah Davis give the volume an authoritative and timely character. The latter's discussion of population, migration, social welfare, and education are especially informative as are Sutter's paper on foreign policy, Scalapino's view of the future, Leng on legal reform, and Barnett's political overview. For that matter, every chapter is outstanding.

Introduction

SHAO-CHUAN LENG

After his rise to power in 1978, Deng Xiaoping launched a new era of economic reform and political liberalization in China. The PRC reform programs, however, have experienced cycles of ups and downs in the past 14 years. The most serious setback was the 1989 Tiananmen tragedy and the repressive measures that followed. More recently, in what may well be his last effort before passing from the scene, Deng has pushed forward with renewed vigor the reform and open-door policies that are resulting in the impressive growth of the Chinese economy.

Still, a number of questions remain to cause general concern. Can the economic reform and growth be sustained? To what extent have changes occurred in political, social, legal, military, and other areas in China? Will the reform programs be able to survive without Deng Xiaoping? Are they truly irreversible? Can a participatory political system be developed in the PRC through peaceful evolution and incremental processes? Can China succeed in doing what neither the U.S.S.R. nor any other Communist society has been able to do—that is, making reform work, modifying its economic and political systems so that they become increasingly effective rather than collapsing? To address these and other related issues, a conference on "Reform and Development in Deng's China" was held at the University of Virginia in November 1992 under the auspices of the Miller Center of Public Affairs. The present volume has grown out of the revised papers presented at the conference.

While the paper-writers hesitate to make firm predictions about the future, they seem to share varying degrees of cautious optimism that reform and change in China will continue beyond Deng Xiaoping. There is a common theme throughout the papers that Communist ideology is increasingly becoming irrelevant in the PRC, giving way to pragmatism and political expediency. Despite some serious problems and difficulties, economic reform and change have had such profound impacts on China that no one can turn back the clock on Deng's reform and open-door policies. As shown in the chapters, changes have also been taking place in other segments of Chinese society. The emergence of economic and social pluralism in China will make future political change inevitable, leading to a more open and participatory polity with more than lip service to the rule of law.

In Chapter one, Professor Doak Barnett starts his "Political Overview" with a succinct review of Deng's reform programs from the late 1970s to the present. He follows that with a discussion of some fundamental differences between the situations in China and those in the Soviet Union and Eastern Europe in the late 1980s, the single most important difference being China's remarkably successful economic growth and development. In post-Tiananmen China, Barnett is particularly impressed by what happened in 1992: the great economic boom, the acceleration of systemic economic reforms, and the victory of reformers in the choice of future leadership and the commitment to market economy and open-door policies made at the 14th Party Congress.

Barnett's overall optimism is somewhat tempered by the current overheated Chinese economy and by the continuation of Chinese leaders' primary concern for the maintenance of political stability over the institution of far-reaching structural changes in the political system. Nevertheless, he sees a wide variety of variables that will affect political evolution in China. Among them are continued economic and social changes, the emerging interest and pressure groups, and the remarkable communication revolution that has profoundly affected all of the Chinese population. In a generation or two, Barnett suggests, various pressures from below, from above, and from outside China will likely move the country from its authoritarian polity to a more pluralistic political system—not a carbon copy of Western democracy but perhaps a "democracy with Chinese characteristics."

Chapter two, written by Professors John Fei and Jack Hou, analyzes the Comprehensive Economic Reform (CER) in Deng's

China since 1978. The paper begins with a survey of the Socialist transformation period (1949-1978) in the PRC to highlight the background of the CER. Then it proceeds to examine in detail Deng's economic reform first in the rural sector (1918-1984) and later in the urban sector (1985-). The major thesis that the authors have developed in this study is that the collapse of socialism in the form of a "Party State" has occurred because it is not compatible with the requirements of modern society as it has developed in the 20th century. Following that, they contend, to complete the CER in the years ahead, a "peaceful evolution" toward capitalism will be inevitable in all ex-socialistic countries including the PRC.

Throughout the chapter, the authors provide useful tables and figures to illustrate their points. Failure of socialist transformation of the Chinese economy is attributable to the unwarranted faith in the irrelevant and faulty theory of Marx. Much time and human energy were wasted on the "noble" and elusive effort to reform human nature by revolutionary political force. The authors have high praise for the rural reform of Deng's CER. They are also basically optimistic about the progress and prospect of China's urban reform, which requires the separation of enterprises from politics and the revival of an interest culture to bring about structural flexibility and a healthy metabolism. A special note is made on the increasing "privatization" of the Chinese economy under CER. The total industrial output in the last five years grew at an average annual rate of 13.24 percent while the private industrial output grew at 44.10 percent. At the same time, the authors believe that the labor or employment issue is the "beast" that the Chinese reformers have to conquer. Between 1978 and 1990, the growth of the labor force was close to 40 percent, compounded by the existence of vast redundant or surplus labor in both the rural and urban sectors.

Like Fei and Hou, many other seasoned observers are also more positive than negative in their appraisals of economic reform in Deng's China.[1] A few recent developments regarding the Chinese economy may be cited as reasons for optimism. First, under Deng's influence, the establishment of a socialist market economy in the PRC has been approved by the 14th Party Congress and the Eighth National People's Congress[2], while an unprecedented economic decentralization has been spread to the country. Second, Deng's policy of accelerating economic growth has been carried out in such a way that in 1992 China enjoyed a 12.8 percent growth in GDP and 21 percent growth in industrial output (with the nonstate sector leading the way).[3] Third, the open-door policy has helped move the Chinese economy toward globalization. In foreign investment, for example, China signed new agreements in 1992 on the utilization of foreign capital involving a total of $68.5 billion, an increase of 250 percent over that of 1991.[4] The value of China's total foreign trade in 1992 was $165.6 billion, doubling that in 1988 and placing China as the 11th largest trading country in the world.[5] Fourth, the accomplishments of Chinese economic reform have received special international recognition. In the spring of 1993, through the use of a new method of calculating purchasing power parity, the World Bank and International Monetary Fund ranked the Chinese economy as one of the three largest in the world.[6]

On the other hand, not to be overlooked are a number of economic problems and difficulties facing Chinese reformers. Among them are the widening gaps between regions and between urban and rural populations, inadequacies of financial and communication systems, weaknesses in energy and raw material industries, and rising corruption and other economic crimes. The most immediate and serious challenge is the overheated economy and the threat of inflation. In the first half of 1993, the country's economy grew at a pace of 14 percent and inflation rose to 21.6 percent in cities.[7] To cope with the situation, Vice Premier Zhu Rongji, a leading reformer, has assumed the additional post of central banker and has announced a program to control inflation, including a further slowdown in bank lending, a call to rein in consumer spending, and the delay of some planned infrastructure projects. Both Western and Chinese commentators tend to agree that this time, as contrasted with 1989, Zhu's more sophisticated approach may be able to bring the economy in for a "soft landing" and to slow the growth to a manageable but still high rate.[8]

In Chapter Three, Professor Deborah Davis discusses Chinese society under Deng. Several issues such as population control, migration, social welfare, and education are chosen for specific examination. It is in those social policy arenas that the author shows the difference between urban and rural developments and the cross-currents of change and continuity that animate contemporary Chinese society. As she points out, the Deng economic reform has dramatically altered China's physical landscape. Yet there have also been important continuities with the Maoist legacy. Fertility has stabilized at the same level as during the late Mao era; generous, universal pensions remain a protected benefit for urban employees; dependence on subsidized public services still persists in Chinese society today.

At the same time, however, important changes coexist with continuities. A one-child family has become the norm in urban China, and large families of five to six children have almost disappeared in the countryside. Rural-urban boundaries have become increasingly blurred, and millions of rural residents move back and forth between village and city. In the larger context of economic growth and change, Davis concludes, Deng's modest and even compromised social reforms, if continued, will have the potential of effecting a more fundamental change of Chinese society in the future than was attempted by the radical transformation program of the past.

Chapter Four, "Legal Reform in Deng's China," contributed by myself, consists of three parts. The first part is concerned with motivations and measures of Deng's legal reform. Obviously, the foremost reason behind the reform has been the need for a secure and orderly environment to develop the Chinese economy and attract foreign interest. Among the major steps taken to build socialist legality with Chinese characteristics are reorganization and expansion of formal legal institutions and enactment of a host of laws and regulations that include organic statutes, criminal and civil codes, and numerous economic laws and regulations.

The second part of the chapter deals with the limits and difficulties confronting the reform. Besides such problems as the shortage of trained personnel, the general skeptical attitude toward law, and bureaucratic abuses of power, the overriding restriction on China's legal development continues to be the dictates of politics. Whenever the Communist regime is perceived to be threatened, legal niceties are set aside. The ways Beijing has treated political dissidents and student demonstrations in general and at Tiananmen in particular are telling illustrations. In the final part of the chapter, the assessment of the latest trends and future prospects is more hopeful. Deng Xiaoping's dramatic push for his reform and open-door policies has helped accelerate the economic growth in China. There is also a more relaxed atmosphere permitting liberal views on legal issues to be expressed openly, even though the PRC's human rights record still has a long way to go to meet international standards. More importantly, Deng's program has brought about a changing economic landscape in China and is creating socio-economic pluralism there, a precondition necessary to the rule of law. One can hope that persistence of Deng's program and continued economic and social changes in the country will pave the way for a gradual but inevitable political change and also accelerate the pace of China's long march to the rule of law.

In Chapter Five, Professor Paul Godwin offers a tentative appraisal of the military reforms directed by Deng Xiaoping in the past 14 years. From its formal initiation in 1978 as the fourth of the Four Modernizations, the modernization of national defense was to have two broad objectives. In the short term, it was to improve the combat effectiveness of the Chinese armed forces. In the long term, it was to create a defense establishment capable of building and maintaining modern military forces and sustaining their requirements for advanced weapons and equipment without undue reliance on foreign technology and suppliers. Using these two closely related and still valid objectives as a frame of analysis, the author proceeds to assess the efforts of China's defense modernization under Deng.

Among the strengths of Chinese military reforms are improvements in creating a trained, technically proficient officer corps and in revamping military strategy, tactics, and operations. The primary strength, according to Godwin, is Deng's long-term defense modernization strategy that will serve China in the 21st century. If carried out with patience, it will provide China with the defense capability and the self-confidence required by a major power to act independently in the international system. There exists a tension, however, between Deng's grand design and the current need perceived by the military for purchasing weapons and equipment from abroad. While definitely favorable toward Deng's strategy, the author also sees its negative effects of hurting the morale of the new officer corps and creating potential problems in absorbing more modern arms and equipment in the future. Thus, in his words, "The purchase of end-use items and the potential for licensed production of Russian arms and equipment could well fulfill multiple needs and represent an adjustment in Deng's strategy for modernizing China's national defense." Such an adjustment is described by the author as a midcourse correction typical of Deng's pragmatic response to reform and modernization.

Chapter Six, written by Dr. Robert Sutter, discusses China in world affairs under Deng Xiaoping. It provides contexts, perspectives, and a comprehensive assessment regarding the issues related to Chinese behavior in the world. In reviewing the development of the PRC foreign policy up to the Tiananmen crackdown, the author points out that in the 1980s China adopted an overall pragmatic approach to world affairs compatible with its program of reform and modernization and with its increasing dependence on the developed countries for assistance, trade, technology, and investment. The massacre at Tiananmen in 1989 and the subsequent collapse of communism in the Soviet bloc are believed to have seriously undermined the prestige and legitimacy of the Beijing regime under Deng, particularly in the West. To Deng's credit, however, China has managed in recent years to "establish cordial or workman-like relations with all countries throughout its periphery"; it also has "used China's location, economic reform policies, and other advantages to place China in seemingly advantageous position for further growth and development in East Asia."

In the author's opinion, whether China will continue its relatively pragmatic and moderate foreign policy in the future depends upon two sets of factors. They are (1) internal stability and reform and (2) interaction of China with key states around its periphery and Chinese adjustment to international trends in the new world order. Turning to the implications of Chinese behavior for American interests and U.S.-China relations, the author shows the Tiananmen crackdown again as a great divide. For two decades, China's behavior in world affairs was seen by Americans as essentially favoring U.S. interests. Since Tiananmen and the end of the Cold War, there have been divided views in the United States about the PRC and U.S.-China relations. Those who think Chinese behavior as compatible with U.S. interests argue for a moderate, accommodating, and engaged American policy toward China, while those who stress the contradictions between Chinese actions and American interests argue for stronger U.S. pressure on China to make changes. Despite his campaign rhetoric, says the author, President Clinton currently appears to be pursuing a more balanced China policy, tougher than Bush's position but flexible enough to preserve growing U.S.-Chinese economic and other relations.

Chapter Seven, "Deng's China—What Lies Ahead?" written by Professor Robert Scalapino, performs the function of a conclusion for the volume. It starts with a succinct survey of economic achievements and problems in Deng's China. Measured against former Soviet bloc countries, China's economic picture is much brighter, partly "because the reforms have been underway for more than a decade" and partly "because this society had an entrepreneurial spirit that could not be eliminated by 40 years of collectivism." Three central issues in the economic realm are listed for the future: development of a rational relationship between state and market; balance between national macroeconomic policies and subnational economic programs, and trimming and reorientation of the massive bureaucracy. Despite the awesome challenges, the author is cautiously optimistic. His reason is that the economic reforms and the goals set for the coming years accord "reasonably well" with China's capabilities.

On Chinese politics, the author's optimism is much more reserved. There are two central political issues in China. One is leadership and the other is the allocation of authority among center, region, province, and locality. Scalapino is encouraged by the composition of the current CCP Politburo that shows China's top leaders being drawn from the well-educated, technocratic class, closely tied to China's key eastern provinces and great metropolitan centers. The question is whether China can do without a paramount leader to hold the country together. As pointed out, the economic reform in China has contributed to very considerable political as well as economic decentralization. Given the decline of

Communist ideology, the PRC leadership tends to stress nationalism, unity, and stability to preserve the national structure. Taking this and other factors into consideration, the author does not see an early movement in China toward a multiparty system or the wide-range freedoms associated with a democratic society. Rather, China seems likely to remain viable as a political entity in the years immediately ahead by "combining political authoritarianism with social and economic pluralism." This Chinese polity, however, is expected to be constantly tested as social and economic diversity and international contacts continue to expand.

ENDNOTES

1. See, for instance, Chu-yuan Cheng, "China's Economy and the CCP 14th Party Congress: New Leap Forward and Consequences" in Bih-Jaw Lin and Gerrit W. Gong (eds.), *Sino-American Relations at a Time of Change* (Washington, D.C.: Center of Strategic & International Studies, 1994), 99-114; "China: The Emerging Economic Powerhouse of the 21st Century," *Business Week*, 17 May 1993, 54-68; Y. C. Yeh, "Macroeconomic Issues in China in the 1990s," *The China Quarterly* 131 (September 1992): 501-544.

2. The Eighth National People's Congress in March 1993 adopted and incorporated the "socialist market economy" into the amendment to the preamble of the PRC Constitution. *Beijing Review* 36 (26 April-2 May 1993): 14-15.

3. Ibid. (8-14 March 1993): 31, 33.

4. Ibid., 37.

5. Ibid. (22-28 February 1993): 5.

6. The World Bank ranked China only after the United States while the International Monetary Fund ranked China behind the United States and Japan. See World Bank, *Global Economic Prospects and the Developing Countries* (Washington, D.C., 1993), 66-67; *New York Times*, 20 May 1993, A1, A8.

7. *Wall Street Journal*, 20 July 1993, A8.

8. *Asian Wall Street Journal*, 6 July 1993, 1, 9; *Business Week*, 19 July 1993, 42-43.

CHAPTER ONE

Political Overview

A. DOAK BARNETT

In politics, setting priorities is always crucial. Leaders must decide which problems are most pressing, which issues should be stressed, and what goals are most important. Deng Xiaoping, who has been China's foremost leader since the late 1970s, has always been clear on what, in his mind, China's highest priority should be: economic development of the country. In the 1980s, as Deng promoted a series of reform programs that he felt were essential to China's economic development, he faced, almost constantly, opposition from other party elders in Beijing who favored more conservative economic policies and slower reform, as well as from Beijing's dwindling and aging group of senior ideologists who fought a losing rear-guard battle to try to preserve as much as they could of Mao's ideological legacy.

Despite opposition, Deng has been able for almost a decade and a half to move China steadily toward some kind of market socialism—and toward greater integration of China into the world economy. Most of the debate within the Chinese leadership about economic reform during these years has not really been about whether some kind of reform is essential; it has focused on questions relating to the pace, extent, and exact nature of the changes that should be made in China's economic system.

During these years, there has been some—although less—debate in China on issues relating to political reform—including debate about the fundamental relationships that exist and should exist between economic and political changes. However, the

1

primary locus of this political debate has not been within the top leadership; it has gone on mainly within small but important groups of urban intellectuals. As economic reform progressed during the 1980s, up until 1989 at least, there were some cautious steps towards limited political liberalization, which briefly speeded up during two periods, when Hu Yaobang and Zhao Ziyang held the post of party general secretary. Most of the party's leaders, however, have seemed to agree with Deng Xiaoping's view that while economic reform should proceed fairly rapidly, political reform, at least in its initial stages, should be carried out only with great caution, should be limited, and should be very gradual. While virtually all the leaders have favored the abandonment of the most totalitarian aspects of the Maoist era, not only Deng but most of his colleagues in the top leadership seem to have been convinced that authoritarian political controls should be maintained for a considerable period of time to prevent the inevitable tensions and dislocations that result from rapid social change and economic reform from creating political instability which, in their view, could threaten to undermine not only the economic reforms but also the regime itself.

Ever since the late 1970s, the process of reform in China has been cyclical. Periods of rapid economic growth and economic reform have been followed by periods of retrenchment and, at times, partial retreat. Periods of some political liberalization have been succeeded by a reassertion of political controls and, periodically, strong repression of all signs of open dissidence. One economic cycle reached its peak in 1988, when rising inflation and a general over-heating of the economy compelled the leadership to adopt a severe economic austerity program, mainly to bring inflation under control—which it did. One political cycle reached its peak in 1989, when there was growing dissatisfaction in China not only among students but also among the general urban population—dissatisfaction that was fueled primarily by rising inflation, growing corruption, and increasing social inequities and cleavages. All of these problems were essentially side effects of the economic reform process. In any case, they erupted in the spring of 1989 in mass demonstrations and culminated in the Tiananmen massacre in Beijing in June.

The shock of that tragedy led some analysts—especially ones in the West, but some in China as well—to proclaim that reform in China was dead and that because of the regime's loss of legitimacy, the Chinese Communists' system would probably soon be replaced by something else—although by what was by no means clear. The subsequent collapse of communist regimes in Eastern Europe, followed by the political disintegration of the Soviet Union, convinced many of these analysts that their initial predictions had been right. Clearly, however, their judgments about the rapid demise of the Beijing regime were wrong. It was true that powerful forces of change had been unleashed in China throughout the 1980s. By the end of the 1980s, it was clear that the processes of change unleashed by these forces were unstoppable and irreversible. These changes, however, did not undermine the regime and cause its collapse, as the changes in the European communist nations had done. In many respects, in fact, the changes enhanced the ability of the regime to adapt to a rapidly changing world and a rapidly changing China.

Economically, by the late 1980s China had reached a halfway house in reforming its economic system. Already, it was far different from what it had been in the Maoist period. Moreover, the momentum of change was still strong and was pushing it forward, beyond its halfway house. Even the critics of reform in China had acknowledged by the end of the 1980s, implicitly if not explicitly, that they had no alternative economic program to offer.

Politically, the underlying, secular trends in the political system during the 1980s clearly were altering the foundations of Chinese political system—changing it from an extreme Maoist form of totalitarianism to a much more decentralized, looser form of liberalized authoritarianism. Following the Tiananmen crisis, political controls were tightened, and strongly repressive measures were taken against dissidents in China. Yet, in the three years since then, the regime has not restored—and indeed has not been able to restore—anything like the pre-reform Maoist totalitarian system. Even conservative leaders have had to recognize that not only is the Maoist system economically and politically incompatible with modernization, but they also have had to accept the fact that they no longer have the capability to reestablish old totalitarian controls

3

like those in earlier decades. They cannot even try to do so without abandoning their most important goals of modernization.

Despite the fact that there were some similarities in the late 1980s between the situation in China and those in the Soviet Union and Eastern Europe, there were also some fundamental differences that made it unlikely that China would follow their path—or that the Communist regime in China faced the specter of imminent collapse of the kind that undermined the European Communists. Over a good many years, it was true, the legitimacy of the Chinese Communist party had been gradually weakened—by the aftereffects of the Great Leap Forward in the 1960s, by the consequences of the Cultural Revolution in the late 1960s and early 1970s, and then by the Tiananmen Square massacre. The regime's legitimacy had not evaporated, however, as it had in Eastern Europe where virtually all communist regimes lacked any strong indigenous roots and in the Soviet Union where prolonged economic stagnation was a fundamental reason for the total collapse of the Communist party's legitimacy. In China, there were still some strong bases of support in the 1980s. The government was bolstered by the economic successes produced by its reform policies. The military establishment remained loyal and supportive of the party-led regime. The majority of China's rural population showed no signs of significant opposition, in large part because their living standards and economic welfare were rapidly improving. Although China faced serious problems in dealing with its minority populations in the western regions of the country, these problems were in no way comparable to those that helped to tear apart the Soviet Union and some East European nations.

The single most important difference between China and the Soviet Union and Eastern Europe was the fact that during the 1980s China's economic growth and development were remarkably successful. Economically, it moved to the forefront of all developing countries in its rate of GNP growth. With ups and downs, the rate averaged 9 to 10 percent a year, which was extraordinary for such a large developing nation. As a result, living standards rose rapidly in China during the 1980s; for most people they doubled or tripled. Moreover, China's economic reforms, despite some temporary retreats, made steady progress—far greater progress than that made

4

in economic reform in any other communist nation—and they were steadily transforming China's economic system. Step by step, China's economy moved toward a much more decentralized and marketized economy—and it became increasingly dynamic. Also, after abandoning the fairly autarchic policies of the late Maoist period, China moved with surprising rapidity to expand its foreign economic relations and integrate the country into the world economy.

For a short period between late 1988 and early 1990, the Chinese economy seemed to be moving backward. It experienced something close to a recession, and the reform process slowed to a crawl. It soon became clear, however, that this was caused by the austerity program adopted in 1988 and *not* as a result of a policy reversal caused by the Tiananmen crisis. By the latter part of 1990, China's economic growth rate began to pick up, and it gained strength in 1991. Movement towards economic reform was resumed. At first, it was halting and piecemeal, and it was still constrained by ongoing disagreement and debate within the top leadership. Then, in early 1992, Deng Xiaoping threw the full weight of his great prestige in favor of accelerated economic reform and faster economic growth, and China's economy "took off." China today is unquestionably the most dynamic economy of any size in the world.

The year 1992 will be remembered in China for several things: the great economic boom of 1992, the demolishing of the last ideological obstacles to economic reform, the acceleration of systemic economic reforms aimed at creating a market economy, and the seemingly decisive victory of economic reformers in the choices for future leadership that were made at the 14th Party Congress in October—a Congress that strongly endorsed Deng's reform program and reshuffled the top leadership to give economic reformers a much clearer predominance over conservatives than at any time in the past.

Very few people in the West paid attention to the 14th Party Congress in October. It was an event that deserved more notice. The Congress obviously did not end, once and for all, all debate on future policy. Nor did it necessarily predetermine the ultimate outcome of the prolonged "rolling succession" that is producing a new leadership in China. Nevertheless, the Congress did ensure that China will move rapidly in the direction that Deng has long been urging—toward a more marketized and more internationalized economy—and it created a new political balance in Beijing's leadership that increased the likelihood that, following the death of Deng and the other remaining party elders, China will continue moving on its present path of economic reform. Since as early as the mid-1980s, I have been convinced that the basic direction of China's present economic reform program has been irreversible. The trends in 1992 and the decisions made at the 14th Party Congress should convince those who have until recently been skeptics.

Some of the specific consequences of the 14th Party Congress deserve mention and comment here. At the Congress the leadership showed great optimism about the Chinese economy—perhaps too much optimism—and endorsed a very rapid rate of GNP growth in the years ahead. There has long been debate in China about what the most appropriate rate should be. For several years, there seemed to be general agreement that perhaps 7 percent was an appropriate long-term rate. As recently as 1990, however, the seeming consensus was that the rate should be somewhat lower, perhaps around 6 percent. In October 1992, however, the Party Congress raised the target rate to between 8 and 9 percent. In my opinion, China's leaders may decide, before long, that this is an unwisely high target. It does not seem to represent sober judgment based on past experience, but instead reflects the extraordinary dynamism of 1992, when an almost runaway pace of growth seemed to be developing. In April 1992 when I visited China, I could already sense that the pace of growth was rapidly escalating—and already some Chinese reform economists I knew were beginning to worry about the danger of inflationary pressures. On my next visit, in October, on the eve of Party Congress, my dominant impression was one of an extraordinary economic dynamism—almost manic efforts on the part of everyone to make money, build, produce, and sell. In one sense, the dynamism that was evident all over the country was exciting. It revealed a new momentum that would drive China's modernization forward more rapidly than anybody thought

6

possible a few years ago, but it also, in my opinion, poses some potential dangers.

What China needs is a steady, sustainable process of economic growth. What it has had since the start of the 1980s has been a pattern of boom and bust. Many of China's leaders and most of its economists have recognized that this pattern poses real problems, and the regime has tried to strengthen its fiscal and monetary mechanisms in order to manage and control the economy more effectively. What seemed to be reappearing in the latter half of 1992 was the danger of inflation that could lead to another bust. Some knowledgeable people in Beijing argued that improved controls and other changes since the inflation of 1988 made the danger of inflation less than what might have appeared on the surface. Others, however, believe that the present rapid rate of growth poses real risk. The rate of GNP growth for the country as a whole will be over 10 percent in 1992, and in some coastal provinces it will be much higher. This is probably too fast, and steps are likely to be taken soon to slow the process down. Another bust could be destabilizing—although probably not so destabilizing that it would undermine the regime or deflect it from its present general course more than temporarily.

The 14th Party Congress also represented the climax of a long process in which Chinese Communist leaders, ever since the death of Mao, have redefined the Party's ideology in order to justify increasing pragmatism and flexibility in devising workable policies to promote economic reform and development. Conservative leaders and ideologues have fought this process of ideological redefinition at every step of the way. Since the end of the 1970s, however, there has been a fairly dramatic decline in the force and relevance of ideology in China. Today, Marxism-Leninism-Mao Zedong Thought has relatively few ardent believers even among the leadership; it is not regarded as very relevant to China's problems by the rising new generation of technocratic leaders; and among China's youth it has almost no credibility at all. The regime clearly faces, therefore, the problem of defining a new set of values that can fill the vacuum created by the weakening of Marxism. For some time the leadership has been trying to do this, and it now is placing increasing emphasis on appeals to Chinese patriotism, on the revival of many traditional Chinese values and ideas, and on pride in modernization and development—as well as appeals to economic self-interest on the basis of steadily rising living standards. Already, it is fairly clear that the main prop of the regime's legitimacy rests, above all, on its economic performance.

Despite these long-term trends and the declining importance of ideology in a traditional sense, however, the leadership has still felt compelled to explain and to justify its fundamental economic policies in ideological terms—or, perhaps it is more accurate to say that Deng and his reformist supporters have felt it necessary to adjust definitions of ideology in ways that could undercut opposition from the critics of reform. This process took a major step in the mid-1980s, when the regime asserted that China would move from a socialist planned economy to a socialist commodity economy. The 14th Party Congress went much further, however, and stated that China would now transform its economy into a socialist market economy. This semantic change may sound unimportant to outsiders. In China, though, it clearly signaled that ideology now sanctions moving very far toward a marketized economy—one not very different from those of non-communist East Asian nations.

Few people in the West realize how far systemic economic change already has gone in China. Today, roughly two-thirds of the economy is no longer subject to centralized state planning, and roughly one-half of the output of even the industrial sector of the Chinese economy now comes not from state-owned enterprises but from urban collectives, township and village enterprises, private enterprises, and joint Chinese-foreign ventures. This trend will clearly continue, and the ideological pronouncements emerging from the 14th Party Congress will make it easier.

The tasks of economic reform that still lie ahead in China are still very difficult. The regime has started, but still has a long way to go, in some crucial tasks: reform of China's large, inefficient, unprofitable state enterprises; completion of price reform and the move from the present multiple price system to a unified price system; further fiscal and monetary reform that will enable the leadership in Beijing to regulate the economy more effectively; and many others. There will be many bumps on the road ahead, and it would be surprising if there were not new crises and setbacks in the

8

1990s. There is little likelihood, however, that these will convince the Chinese that they should try to move backward to restore a command economy or to turn inward economically.

The 14th Party Congress produced a new leadership and marked another major stage in the long post-Mao succession process that will only be completed when Deng Xiaoping and all the other elder members of his revolutionary generation are gone. Although well advanced, the succession process is not yet *totally* finished—but it is now *almost* finished. There will probably be further changes resulting from the National People's Congress meeting in 1993, but that could well be the last occasion in which Deng and other elders will be able to have a decisive effect on the choice of leaders. Certainly Deng and the others are not likely to survive until the next Party Congress in 1997.

Since the early 1980s, a new kind of leadership has been emerging in China—one that is essentially technocratic and pragmatic and relatively little influenced by old ideological dogmas or early revolutionary traditions. In 1988, when I traveled extensively through 19 provinces in China and met many local leaders at all levels, I concluded that at the provincial and lower levels a sweeping generational change had already, by then, produced a new kind of leadership in almost every place I visited—except at the very top, among the small group of Party elders in Beijing. By the end of the 14th Party Congress, the leadership change was near-complete in Beijing, too.

The Party Congress abolished the Central Advisory Commission, the last institutional bastion of old conservatives, and it reshuffled all the top decision-making bodies within the party in ways that strengthened the reformers and technocratic leaders in the successor generation. In the highest decision-making body in China, the Standing Committee of the Politburo, four members continued without change: General Secretary Jiang Zemin, Premier Li Peng, Qiao Shi, and Li Ruihuan. Two members who were generally regarded to be the conservatives in a Standing Committee most closely associated with conservatives among the Party elders were retired: Yao Yilin and Song Ping. Most important, three new members were appointed, and all of them were strong supporters of economic reform: Zhu Rongji, the former mayor of Shanghai;

9

Liu Huaqing, a military leader who was aging but was strongly associated with reform; and Hu Jintao, a former protege of Hu Yaobang who also has been strongly associated with the reformers. Of the seven members now in the Standing Committee, only Li Peng has a reputation that tends still to link him to the most conservative party elders, and during the past year and a half it has become increasingly evident that even he has adjusted to the changing situation and now gives strong support to Deng's current party line.

Both the Politburo as a whole and the Central Committee, the largest of the top decision-making bodies, have also undergone major changes. In the Politburo, eight former members were dropped, and with the infusion of new blood, it is clear that younger technocrats are now predominant; one-half of them are men with engineering educations. The coastal provinces, which have been in the forefront of economic reform, now have strong representation in the Politburo. Among the Politburo's present membership are the party secretaries of Shanghai, Tianjin, Shandong Province, and Guangdong Province. Although Liu Huaqing, the military's representative in the Standing Committee, comes from the elder generation, he clearly is a symbol of professionalization and modernization. In the Central Committee as a whole, close to half of the membership has changed, and as a result, better-educated technocrats are now clearly predominant (close to 85 percent of them are college graduates).

The changes in China's top leadership made at the 14th Party Congress clearly has strengthened the position of reformers, weakened the position of conservatives, and substantially increased the possibility of not only a continuation of reform policies but also a relatively smooth succession period. There is no guarantee, however, that the leadership now in place will last for the next five years—as, they are intended to in theory. When Deng and all the other elders finally pass from the scene, a very new situation will be created. Virtually all of the present leaders who hold the highest institutional posts in China have risen to the top with the support of one or more of the Chinese Communist's surviving Founding Fathers—Deng, Chen Yun, or one or more of the other elders. When all of these elders have gone, the members of the next generation will have to build their own bases of support, create their own coalitions, and prove that they can lead without their original political patrons. Some of the members of the present Standing Committee and Politburo probably will prove to be able leaders, while others will probably prove to be transitional figures. Yet, whoever the specific leaders surviving in the immediate post-Deng era are, the essential characteristics of the present leadership—and their technocratic, pragmatic, nonideological predispositions—are not likely to change. In the 1990s, China's leadership will be dominated by men (there are not many women among the group) who are committed above all to comprehensive economic reform, rapid economic growth, and the full integration of China into the international economic system. This kind of leadership will almost certainly last for the next five years, probably it will survive for the rest of this century, and possibly it will continue well into the next century.

This is not to suggest that there will be an end to political debates and conflicts over economic policies. The intrinsic difficulties of reforming and developing a country as large and as complex as China are such that there are no clear answers to what will be an endless progression of old as well as new problems. Nevertheless, the arena for future political battles is likely to be one in which old ideological conflicts are almost irrelevant, and the main controversies are likely to be less over policy aims than over how best to achieve national goals.

What does all of this mean about the future of political reform in China—and about the likely nature of the Chinese political system in the period immediately ahead?

There is little prospect in the immediate future for rapid progress toward institutional change that could move the country toward real democratization. Deng Xiaoping and those closest to him still insist on giving priority to the maintenance of political stability—and Deng himself insists on his "four cardinal principles" and the continuation of one-party rule. None of the top leaders is now prepared to give serious consideration to allowing opposition parties, a really free press, or the genuinely competitive election of top leaders. In varying degrees, most of the present top leaders, including the most dedicated economic reformists, seem—at least at

11

the present moment—to endorse the idea that strong political control is essential to ensure the stability that they believe to be a requirement for continuing economic reform and development. There continue to be some pressures from below—especially from intellectuals—for more far-reaching political changes, even though in the post-Tiananmen situation they cannot openly promote democratic ideas. Still, even among China's intellectuals, there are many who put a high premium on political stability, favor only gradual political reform, and endorse what is called the idea of "neo-authoritarianism," as a transitional form of polity during the early stages of economic reform. Supporters of "neo-authoritarianism" argue that democratization can and will develop later, but only when economic development and social change have made more progress. One reason that so many people in China, including reformers, put such a high premium on stability is their memory of the chaos of the Cultural Revolution, as well as the near-breakdown of the political system in 1989. The chaos in the Soviet Union following the collapse of communism there has reinforced the view of a great many Chinese that while economic reform can move ahead rapidly, political reform must be cautious and incremental to avoid instability leading to chaos.

For many Chinese, the term *neo-authoritarianism* really refers to Taiwan, or South Korea, or possibly Singapore. The experience in these places, especially Taiwan, are seen by many, including some top Chinese leaders, as providing a model for China—a distinctive "Asian" path to reform, in which economic reform and growth come first, major changes in society follow, and political pluralization leading to ultimate democracy comes later, with a lag of perhaps 20 or 30 years. Is this a feasible path for China's political development in the period ahead? That remains to be seen. It is the path, however, that many Chinese leaders believe they should try to follow.

It is easy to describe a wide variety of variables that will affect the actual political evolution of China in the post-Deng period—and, also, a fairly wide range of possible political outcomes. Rating them on a scale of probability is difficult, however, and I will not attempt to do so here. Instead, I will outline what I believe, in light of the present situation and current trends in China, is a very plausible, in

12

fact likely, direction for political change in the Chinese system in the immediate period ahead.

There is a high likelihood that the Chinese Communist party will continue to have the capacity to maintain its rule—so long as the Chinese economy continues to develop at a reasonable rate and the basic policies for economic reform result in overall progress. The nature of the party, however, which already has changed a great deal in recent years, will doubtless continue to change. Its prestige as a political institution and its real power have steadily declined, and this is likely to continue. Increasingly, the party will be forced to share power not only with other institutions in the political structure but also with nonparty and nongovernment organizations and institutions.

The Chinese leadership will almost certainly continue to give top priority to the maintenance of political stability, and judged by Western standards, real political reform will probably lag quite far behind economic reform. It also seems likely, however, that the kind of technocratic leadership that has emerged will before very long move cautiously to resume the kind of incremental political liberalization that was beginning to change the Chinese polity in the middle and latter 1980s up to the Tiananmen crises.

The first steps in that direction may well involve nothing more than renewed efforts to carry out internal reform of China's bureaucracies, which General Secretary Jiang Zemin called for at the 14th Party Congress. This, however, could soon lead to the kind of political liberalization that first Hu Yaobang and then Zhao Ziyang (and his principal adviser on political reform, Bao Tong) actively promoted because they believed that economic modernization required cautious political liberalization. During the periods that Hu and Zhao tried to move political liberalization forward, a wide range of significant changes got underway—and they probably will resume in the post-Deng period. They included: extensive decentralization of decision-making authority (something that has continued, in fact, even since 1989); a significant loosening of political controls (which the Tiananmen crisis brought to a temporary halt); opening China to a remarkable degree to influence from abroad; cautious movement toward greater press freedom, which reached a peak just on the eve of the Tiananmen crisis; a

13

decision to reduce the intervention by the party into both governmental operations and enterprise management; efforts to increase innerparty democracy; definite progress toward building a legal system (despite the continuation of huge flaws in the criminal justice system); growing permissiveness in regard to the flow of information of all kinds throughout society; encouragement of open discussion of national problems and policy options (which was quite remarkable on the eve of Tiananmen); and some experimentation in the choice of local leaders in elections with multiple candidates. Such trends are likely to resume, probably before very long after the party elders are gone. In some areas, one can see renewed movement already.

Nevertheless, the Chinese leadership will probably continue to oppose, for a considerable period of time, any more far-reaching structural changes in the political system. It will also probably attempt to nip in the bud any signs of significant organized political opposition groups emerging. Their ability to do this indefinitely, however, is likely to decline, and there will be growing pressures to take more significant steps toward political reform-pressures from below, from the great changes that are taking place in Chinese society; pressures from above from some of the new technocratic leaders who will increasingly argue that further political changes are necessary for economic development; and pressures from outside the country, from the international community that will continue to criticize China's human rights violations and press it to go further to accommodate international norms.

The rapidity of social change as well as economic development in China in the past decade-plus has been astonishing, and continued social change will inevitably lead to a growing pluralism in society, which will result in increased pressures leading toward gradual political reform. In my own travels all over the country in 1988, I saw far-reaching social changes affecting even the most remote corners of the country, and in the several visits since Tiananmen, I have seen how the social changes are continuing unchecked and are promoting a rapid transformation of the society that eventually will produce broader political change. If space permitted, there are a great many social changes with potential

14

political significances worth discussing. In my limited space, I will mention a few.

Economic reform has created, and continues to create, new groups in China of potential political importance. These include a large and growing group of active entrepreneurs and economic interest groups of a variety of sorts. They are already beginning to assert their own interests and to organize. In the future, this will increasingly affect the political process. Apart from economic groups, there are many other signs of the growth of pluralism in many different sectors of Chinese society. The old Maoist pattern of close party control of the society, through party-led mass organizations that intruded into and attempted to manage every segment of society, has been steadily eroded. Many of the mass organizations are much weaker than they were. Some are beginning to be transformed into interest groups of various kinds. In addition, there has been a reemergence in the post-Mao period of a great many associations and groups of a wide variety of sorts that enjoy varying degrees of autonomy—professional groups, religious groups, new research organizations, foundations of various kinds, and so on. Among China's specialists, there are different views on the importance of such trends. I believe they are of great importance and in time will have a large political impact.

Intellectuals in China were greatly stimulated by the loosening of controls and the opening to the outside world in the 1980s, and before the Tiananmen crisis there was lively debate about China's future development and reform. Since 1989, such debate has been impossible, and politically the intellectuals have been muzzled. The effects of the clampdown, however, are really superficial. Privately, intellectuals continue to speak out with remarkable frankness and criticize the regime with relatively few inhibitions. In this respect, the situation is very different from that in the Maoist period. At some point, intellectuals will find means of speaking out publicly again, and post-Deng leaders will probably feel compelled to loosen controls once again. The regime needs the talent of China's intellectuals. In the 1980s it recognized that greater freedom of expression was necessary to mobilize those talents, and this will be true again, although one cannot predict exactly when. Journalists, too, were pushing the limits of freedom of expression in the period just before Tiananmen, and they, too, have also been muzzled since 1989. But they will again begin to press for greater opportunities for freer expression in the post-Deng period.

In broad terms, there has been a remarkable revolution of rising expectations in China since the late 1970s. It has been fueled by rapid economic growth and the rising living standards that have improved almost everyone's livelihood since the reform process began. This revolution of rising expectations compels the leadership to do its best to meet those expectations, and Chinese leaders now recognize that failure to do so will erode their ability to rule. This fact exerts strong pressure from the population as a whole on the leadership.

As mentioned earlier, the force of Marxist ideology has steadily weakened, and as a result many of the old fetters that posed huge obstacles to change have almost disappeared. This means that despite the retrogression since 1989, there is much more variety in the ideas circulating in China than there was in the past. This is particularly true of China's youth. The younger generation that has grown up in the years since China's "opening" and reform began in the late 1970s clearly live in a very different world—literally—from that of their parents and earlier generations. They are now demanding that China emulate and catch up with the more developed nations, particularly those in East Asia, but also those in the West.

All of China's population, young and old, has been profoundly affected by the remarkable communication revolution that has taken place in the last decade. The outreach not only of radio but also of television to virtually the entire population has linked the most remote areas of China with its major cities and with the outside world to an unprecedented extent. Urban areas, moreover, are now more closely interlinked by telephones, fax machines, duplicating machines, telexes, and so on, than was ever the case in the past. As a result, there has been an explosion of information flows throughout China that has ended, once and for all, the previous isolation of a large majority of the Chinese people. Even though the newest media are politically controlled and even though the controls have been tightened since 1989, the messages that the media carry are powerful forces for change. Perhaps the most powerful message of all is simply the idea that China can, and must, try to catch up with the most advanced areas of the world.

No one can know exactly how or when the rapid economic and social changes that are transforming Chinese society will begin to move the country toward more rapid political reform and start to transform its current authoritarian polity into a more pluralistic political system. Still, there is no doubt that the varied pressures from below, from above, and from outside China will move the country toward greater political reform. The process, however, is likely to be gradual—unless China were to experience major economic failure, in which case the country would probably move not toward democratization, but instead toward chaos or, as a result of a political backlash, to some more authoritarian regime, possibly under a military leadership. What seems most likely is that China will move, with ups and downs, gradually toward political liberalization and toward limited systemic change. Even assuming this is the case, the process will be difficult. Political change in recent decades has been extremely difficult in almost all modernizing, developing societies. Moreover, in China the resulting political system is not likely to be a carbon copy of any Western political system. It is quite possible, however, that in a generation or two, China could develop what might be called "democracy with Chinese characteristics," just as it is now developing what Deng calls "socialism with Chinese characteristics."

China today is like a man on a moving bicycle: It has to keep moving simply to avoid falling down. The general direction of its movement is clear, and the transformation of China's economy will lead to enormous changes in Chinese society that will produce growing pressures for accelerated political reform. The new generation emerging to leadership in China will recognize this; some of them already do. What prevents them from moving more rapidly toward political reform is, above all, their fear of instability. That fear will probably continue to be an obstacle to far-reaching political reform for a fairly long period of time. Nevertheless, new leaders will probably feel it necessary before long to resume movement toward political liberalizations and to seek for ways to do so while avoiding the danger of chaos.

CHAPTER TWO

The Comprehensive Economic Reform of the PRC (1978-)

JOHN C. H. FEI AND JACK W. HOU

Introduction

It has been more than 70 years since the October Revolution in Russia that ushered in the socialistic experiments as inspired by the theory of "scientific socialism" (that is, a conviction in the inevitability of the evolution of matured capitalism into "communism" through "socialism") of Karl Marx, an intellectual of the 19th century. The experiment was carried out in the name of a revolution (based on a noble dedication to the cause of constructing an ideal human society on earth in the remote future) under the leadership of the Communist party in a Leninist party-state. The socialistic experiment spread from Europe to Asia after the Second World War, giving birth to the PRC in 1949. After an initial socialistic transformation period of some 30 years (1949-1978), the PRC went all out for comprehensive economic reform after 1978. It is the purpose of this paper to analyze the experience of China's comprehensive economic reform (CER) under Deng Xiaoping that has, by now, acquired a short history of some 14 years (1978-1992).

Epoch-making events have occurred in rapid sequence since 1989—the Tiananmen massacre, the collapse of the Berlin Wall, the liberalization of socialistic regimes in Eastern Europe, and finally, the disintegration of the mighty U.S.S.R. into a loose union of republics—that were quite unexpected even to the experts on socialistic countries. These events shocked the world and provided strong inductive evidence that the noble socialistic experiment is finally coming to an end. It will take the historian of many generations in the future to discover the cause for the "rise and fall of the socialistic experiments" and to learn from the lessons of history. Our paper is only a modest beginning.

The Chinese experience analyzed in this paper is far from being an isolated event. The CER in the PRC is but a closing chapter of the "Rise and Fall of the Socialistic Experiment" or equivalently, "The Closing of the Case of Karl Marx," for it becomes increasingly clear that the "blueprint" for the ideal society (as outlined, for example, in Marx's *Communist Manifesto* in 1848) was a utopian dream that never had even the slightest chance of successful implementation from the very beginning of its inception. A thesis that we will develop in this paper is that the collapse of socialism in the form of a party-state occurred because it is not conducive to the requirements of modern society in its 20th-century form. Therefore, to complete the CER in the years ahead, a "peaceful evolution" toward capitalism will be inevitable in all ex-socialistic countries including the PRC.

The CER is, we hope, a peaceful evolution process toward—as described in the literature—liberalization, privatization, marketization, decollectivization, and monetization. The complexity of these descriptive characterizations suggests that the CER is an "institution evolutionary process" involving changes in the modes of social/political/economic organization with a scope far broader than the reform of a narrowly defined economic organization based on the centralism of planning and command. An interdisciplinary framework of reasoning is essential for the analysis and interpretation of the CER and of the PRC. Although this evolution process in the PRC shares certain common characteristics with the reform experiences of other socialist countries, the CER, being a unique historical experience of China, is bound to have certain special characteristics which, as conditioned by traditional institutional and cultural values that are peculiarly Chinese, are unlikely to be shared by the de-socialization process of other socialistic countries, such as Russia. Our interests in the CER of the PRC is due primarily to the fact that it has certain characteristics that are uniquely Chinese and yet also entails a fund of transferable historical experiences that can be useful to other socialistic countries in transition. The unique characteristic of the CER will be presented in section IV after the general characteristics are explored first.

We shall begin with a succinct summary of the socialistic transformation period (1949-78) in the PRC to highlight the background of the CER. What should be stressed are three perspectives—historical, spatial, and political in nature—that we feel are absolutely essential for the interpretation of the CER (section I). When Chinese socialism is analyzed in this way, the division of CER into two components—an urban reform and a rural reform—follows naturally. We shall argue that such a "bifocal" framework of analysis (that is, one that contains a rural reform component and an urban reform component) derived from the Chinese experience can be applied to all socialistic countries (e.g., Russia) under reform (section II).

It is then a relatively easy matter to demonstrate the thesis that the disintegration of socialistic experiments will be inevitable by stressing the notion that something went wrong in the missionary vision of Marxian ideology from the very beginning (section III). In section IV the uniqueness of the rural reform experience of China will be commented upon in the light of the above common framework of reasoning. This will be followed by the speculated prospects of urban reform in the PRC (section V). Due to the inevitable "privatization" of the economy in the process of the CER, a brief discussion of China's private sector productivity will be put forth in the last section (section VI). We conclude the paper by reflecting on Keynes' eloquent defense of capitalism at the darkest moment of the depressive thirties.

I. Socialistic Transformation (1949-78): Background for CER in PRC

The background of CER can be traced to the highly politicized economic system—based on the centralism of planning and

21

command–that emerged in mainland China after 30 years of "socialistic transformation" (1949-78). In this process, the prewar system of markets and private property rights (as well as the cultural values that supported these time-honored institutions for well over 1,000 years) were annihilated by the brutality of the political force inspired by an ideology (i.e., Marxism) that was entirely alien to China. Indeed, the CER after 1978 may be viewed as a revival of a long tradition of "historical continuity" after a 30-year (1949-78) interruption that was abrupt, artificial, alien, and brief.

The significance of socialistic transformation will be examined from a historical perspective, a spatial perspective, and a political perspective that are essential for the identification of those characteristics relevant to our interpretation of the CER.

1.1 Historical Perspective

From a long-run historical perspective, the Industrial Revolution that occurred in England toward the last quarter of the 18th century terminated centuries of agrarianism (based on settled agriculture) and ushered in what was referred to by Kuznets (1966) as the epoch of modern economic growth (EMG) in which the growth promotion force became centered in the routinized exploration of the frontier of science and technology and the application of the knowledge so explored as the most essential part of the art of production. This modern way of life proved to be irresistible as, during the course of the last 200 years, the EMG spread spatially and gradually conquered almost all agrarian civilizations in different parts of the globe.

A transition growth process is started during a relative short period (of some 50 years) that represented the termination of the epoch of agrarianism and the initiation of the modern epoch. For England, the transition occurred over the 50-year period 1770-1820, while for Japan, it occurred between 1870-1920. In this historical perspective, the period after the Second World War (1950-) was a transition period for all contemporary LDCs (less-developed countries) on the path toward the modern epoch—following the historical footsteps of all the DCs (developed countries) in the 19th century and the earlier part of the 20th century.

The demand for modernization via "Mr. science and technology" was sloganized in China after the May 4th movement in the 1920s. The transition from agrarianism to the modern epoch began in earnest after the Second World War. It is well known by now that of all contemporary LDCs, a region surrounding mainland China (Taiwan, Hong Kong, Singapore, and South Korea) has been most successful in transforming into a "technology-oriented stage of growth" (based on the export of technology-intensive products) following the footsteps of Japan.[1]

In sharp contrast, during the socialistic transformation period (1949-78) in the PRC, much time and human energy were wasted on the "noble" and elusive cause to reform human nature by revolutionary political force. Thus, in a historical perspective, a basic purpose of CER after 1978 is the economic modernization of China. The purpose is to be realized by constructing an institutional environment conducive to the exploration of science and technology which, indeed, was sloganized as the chief objective of reform by the PRC reformers.[2] A brief examination of the historical performance in terms of growth rates will demonstrate this point (table 1). A word of caution to the reader: Though China has (downwards) "adjusted" the historical performance (pre-1978), many still doubt whether it is a significant exaggeration.

1.2 Political Perspective

Transition of contemporary LDCs from agrarianism toward EMG after 1950 took place in the context of anticolonialism. With rare exception (e.g., Hong Kong), almost all contemporary LDCs, stirred up by a newfound sense of "patriotic nationalism," aspired to achieve economic modernization via an institutional arrangement that tolerated, even encouraged, the employment of the political force to interfere with the operation of the market system. The postwar period witnessed the spectacles of the mushrooming of "economic planning commissions," even for LDCs in the "capitalistic camp" (e.g., in Taiwan and South Korea).[3] Although the politicization of the economic institution had taken on an extreme form as a result of the socialistic transformation in the PRC, it is certainly not a surprise given the political reality of anticolonialism in the postwar era.

TABLE 1

Average Annual Growth Rate
(1952 as Base Year)

FYP	Period	Total		Agri.	Ind.	Const.	Trans.	Comm.
1	1953–57[1]	8.9[2]	(6.6)[3]	3.7	19.6	19.4	11.9	8.0
2	1958–62	-3.1	(-2.6)	-5.8	1.8	-7.8	-0.5	-4.3
0[4]	1963–65	14.7	(11.9)	11.5	21.4	20.9	15.1	2.9
3	1966–70	8.3	(5.7)	3.0	12.3	8.0	5.5	9.3
4	1971–75	5.5	(3.9)	3.5	8.3	5.2	5.3	2.1
5	1976–80	6.0	(4.8)	2.2	8.5	6.9	4.0	7.7
6	1981–85	9.7	(8.6)	9.9	9.2	9.7	9.5	12.4
7	1986–90	7.5	(5.9)					
ST1	1953–77	6.2	(5.5)	2.3	11.3	7.7	6.7	3.8
ST2	1953–77	5.0	(3.5)	-0.1	10.0	5.9	5.5	3.9
ST3	1953–77	7.4	(5.3)	1.6	12.4	9.9	7.3	6.3
ST4	1966–77	6.8	(4.8)	2.6	9.4	6.0	5.3	5.6
CER	1978–85	8.3	(7.2)	7.8	10.1	9.9	8.2	11.5
CER	1978–90	8.0	(6.7)					

Notes: [1]Periodization based on China's Five-Year Plans (FYI).
[2]Average annual growth rate of real national income.
[3]Estimated average annual growth rate of real *per capita* national income.
[4]Recovery period.

Legend: ST1: Socialistic Transformation.
ST2: ST1, excluding the capitalistic style recovery period.
ST3: ST1, excluding the Great Leap and Three Bad Years (1958–62).
ST4: Socialistic Transformation during the Cultural Revolution.
CER: Comprehensive Economic Reform (Capitalistic Transformation).

Source: *Statistical Yearbook of China, 1986*
China Statistical Abstract, 1990
International Financial Statistics, 1992 Yearbook

In the PRC, the politicized economic system is such that the government-society relation is characterized by a totalitarianism that virtually annihilated the "privatized civilian society." In the dual polity of the Leninist party-state, the State Council (with all its planning and economic commissions and line ministries) is responsible for the formation and the execution of the "real material balanced" (contained in the central plan) by bureaucratic command. At the same time, the party apparatus of the party-state exercises vast political power for the purpose of manufacturing a new set of socialistic moral principles through the brutality of coercive political force.

Given this political background, a basic purpose of the CER can be viewed as a liberalization process abstractly defined as the atrophy (or the withdrawal) of arbitrary political forces that are interfering with the social economic life of the population. Thus, "liberalization" amounted to the attempt to rehabilitate a privatized "civilian society" independent of the political force.[4]

In view of the "duality" of the polity before 1978, the CER has two natural components. On the one hand, there is the necessity to rehabilitate the market system (annihilated by socialistic transformation) to take the place of the bureaucratic State Council's centralism of command in the coordination of the economic activities with an impersonal automaticity and impartiality. On the other hand, there is the need to separate the party components from the social economic life that, in fact, no longer serve any positive socio-economic purpose when revolution gave way to experimental pragmatic evolution. The resistance by the party component to relinquish its vested interests in "the power to rule" is, however, only a short-run problem that will be overcome in the years ahead by the "encroachment of ideas" (i.e., the idea that socialism will not work). We can safely predict that in the CER in PRC in the years ahead, the "ideology" will be separated from "politics"—in the same sense that the Church was separated in the West.

1.3 Spatial Perspective

In analyzing the transition from agrarianism (based on settled agriculture) toward the modern epoch (based on science and technology) it is absolutely essential to emphasize a spatial (or locational) persecutive. Under agrarianism, the agriculture and small-scale nonagricultural activities (transportation, commerce, traditional labor-intensive manufacturing) are spatially and dispersedly located to form the rural majority (approximately 80 percent of the total population in the case of the PRC) in villages and small towns. In a juxtaposition, there is the spatially and concentratedly located urban population that constitutes a "vital minority" (approximately 20 percent) living in the large urban centers (such as Peking, Shanghai, Tientsen, and the state capitals in the PRC). The art of production in the urban sector is characterized by those that are typical for the large-scale factories making use of modern science and technology.

The urban-rural dichotomy in the spatial sense is a key conceptual distinction for an analytical treatment of CER from both political and economic standpoints. From an economic standpoint, with the arrival of the epoch of modern growth, the exploration of the frontiers of science and technology essentially takes place in and originates from the urban centers where active human contacts are made and the exchange of ideas takes place. It was always through a process of spatial extension that the forces of modernization (i.e., the modern factory produced seeds, fertilizers, tractors, knowledge) were extended spatially from the urban centers to the "rural backyard." Through an urban-rural interaction, the forces of modernization were transmitted spatially to the rural sector.

From a political standpoint, transition growth in the LDCs in the postwar period has been penetrated by a political force with a "pro-urban bias," which discriminates against the rural population—especially the farmers—due to the political sensitivity of the urban populations (consisted of the intellectuals, the laborers, and the entrepreneurial class). For LDCs in the capitalistic camp (e.g., Taiwan, South Korea, etc.), a host of macro-policies (e.g., policies on tariff protection, foreign exchange rates, money and interest rates) have been adopted to augment the profit and/or income of the urban classes at the expense of the rural population.

There were no exceptions to this "pro-urban bias" in the socialistic countries that seek to extract an "agriculture surplus" (to sustain the urban sector) at terms of trade highly unfavorable to the farmers. In the late 1950s, when the communes were formed in the PRC, the overwhelming majority of the more than 20 million people that were starved to death were from rural populations, which is a concrete indication, in terms of human life, of the pro-urban bias in socialistic China.

II. Urban and Rural Reforms in PRC

The CER of the last 14 years has left behind a major conceptual idea, namely, that the "total" or comprehensive economic reform in socialistic countries consists of two distinct components—an urban reform and a rural reform—that serve different purposes from the historical perspective of transition growth.[5] Chronologically for the PRC, the economic reform first occurred in the rural sector (1978-84) and was later extended to the urban sector (after 1985)—as formally announced in 1984. Let us describe these components in an operational perspective as shown in figure 1.

2.1 Rural Reform

In the transition growth process, the urban-rural interactions took place between the urban sector (containing the State Enterprises on the top and the urban working families at the bottom) on the left-hand side and the rural sector (containing the agricultural and rural industries in the production sector on top, and the rural families below) on the right. The two-way-interaction centers on the exchange of an agricultural surplus (A_s) to feed the urban population for modern factory-produced products—that is, incentive goods (C_A) such as textiles and agriculture inputs (such as fertilizers) as well as capital goods for rural industries (I'). Thus, the modern inputs and technology are "extended" spatially via a

FIGURE 1

Operation of Dualistic Economy

(Post Reform, 1978-)

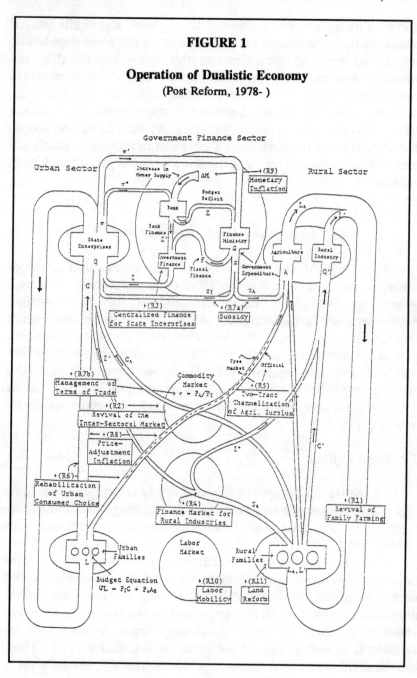

process of urban-rural exchange governed by intersectoral terms of trade to raise the agricultural productivity of the "rural backyard" that, in turn, will have to serve the historical mission to fuel the expansion of the urban sector in the transition growth process. This development of a dualistic economy in transition is applicable to lesser-developed countries in either the capitalistic or socialistic camp.

While the transition growth process, through which the agricultural sector is modernized in an LDC, is a complex issue, it is abundantly clear that the attempt to raise agricultural productivity via urban-rural contact is *the* prerequisite—that is, the only way—for the successful completion of the transition growth process.[6]

Before 1978, the urban-rural interaction in the PRC was organizationally accommodated by the collectivism of communes at the microscopic level of production organization and the centralized planning at the macroscopic level of urban-rural exchange. This socialistic mode of China's institutional arrangement was calculated to politically guarantee consumption welfare for the urban working class via the adoption of a strategy that discriminated against the rural population with unfavorable terms of trade that exploited farmers in the urban-rural exchange.

When viewed in light of this background, the purpose of rural reform is to achieve agricultural modernization—namely, increased agricultural productivity—via a marketization process that signifies the atrophy of the following:

1. collectivism of production in the communes;
2. centralism of command in the urban-rural exchange;
3. political guaranteeism for urban consumption by the restoration of free choice;
4. pro-urban bias that exploited the rural population.

These measures (as will be discussed in section IV) are essentially what will be necessary to achieve agricultural modernization and to allow the agricultural sector to fulfill its historical mission in the transition growth process. Until the time arrives when the transition growth process is completed and the status of the agricultural sector is reduced to that of an appendage to the

29

industrial sector, these measures will be necessary. While the agricultural sector is exploited in all LDCs, it is invariably subsidized in all matured economies. During the transition growth process, agricultural modernization has been a particularly important development bottleneck factor.

A casual examination of China's agricultural productivity will certainly demonstrate the accomplishments of rural reform. Table 2 compares the average annual growth rates of several major crops between the pre- and post-CER periods. It is apparent that the growth of grain stayed steady. This reflects several facts: First, the original grain targets were already close to maximum limits; second, the official tract still retains high priority on grain quotas/contracts; and finally, the accelerated loss of arable land.[7] The lower (though still growing at impressive rates) growth rates of tobacco and hemp are important urban consumption goods and industrial inputs and reflect the original pro-urban/industry strategy. The remainder—categorical nonfood, consumption-oriented agricultural goods—shows the effect of consumerism. The general slowdown after 1986 reflects the potential fact that agricultural production is approaching its limits.

TABLE 2

Agricultural Productivity: Pre- and Post-1978

Average Annual Growth Rates (%)	Grain	Cotton	Oil Seeds	Sugar Cane	Sugar Beet	Tobacco	Hemp
1970–78	3.4	-0.4	2.1	4.6	3.1	12.8	17.5
1978–86	3.3	10.4	13.6	12.8	15.4	9.3	9.6
1987–90	2.2	7.2	3.2*	3.9	–	–	-3.9
1991	2.8	26.7	1.9*	15.1	14.8	–	–
Historical Best	4.2 (1966–70)	4.7 (1953–57)	1.8 (1971–75)	9.4 (1953–57)			

Source: Figures for 1970–86 comes from table 4 (p. 600) in Walker (1989).

Figures for 1987–90 are deduced from the *Statistical Yearbook of China, 1991* (State Statistical Bureau, China).

Figures for 1991 are from the statistical communique of the State Statistical Bureau, 28 February 1992.

"Historical Best" are adapted from Ash (1992).

*Does not include oil from soybeans.

2.2 Urban Reform

The urban production sector (shown on the left-hand side of figure 1) is far more complex than the rural production sector because of the spatially and concentratedly located pattern of the capital-intensive, large-scale production units and the multiplicity of products they produce. The key characteristic of a modern urban sector, however, is the flexibility of the production structure, as can be seen from what may be referred to as a healthy metabolism—that is, the timely birth of new products and the timely death of products that become obsolete—which is indeed essential, unavoidable, and desirable for a technologically dynamic society in the modern epoch. The fact that structural flexibility is the *sine qua non* of a modern society can be seen from the products-cycles of Hong Kong and Japan or from the fact that in a normal prosperous year, tens of thousands of firms and products in the United States will go bankrupt and disappear from the market as a result of the natural selection which takes place in a healthy modern society.

To accommodate the requirement of structural flexibility of the modern epoch, the mode of organization of the urban economy must be designed in such a way that the allocation of investment funds to the multitude of large-scale enterprises (state enterprises under socialism or corporations under capitalism) can ensure a healthy metabolism. As a general rule, for capitalism or socialism, the industry and firms that are deprived of funds of investment finance to acquire capital goods will die. A key organizational weakness of the socialistic economy (one that was heralded, ironically, as evidence of the superiority of socialism in the PRC before 1978) was that investment funds were allocated centrally by the bureaucrats so that no industry or firm would ever be granted a "death certificate" no matter how erroneously the investment funds were allocated. The logical consequence of a politically guaranteed nonfailure of all industries and firms is structural rigidity, a malady that is common to all centrally planned socialistic economies.

The history of the experiments with socialism and the apparent failure of communism have led to an inescapable conclusion that all-people-owned state enterprises in the urban production sector is not accommodative of the healthy metabolism required for a modern economy. With this background in mind, the basic purpose of urban reform is to enhance structural flexibility (that is, to ensure a healthy metabolism) for the large-scale modern, state enterprises in the urban sector.

In the PRC, for example, after 14 years of CER, a bankruptcy law is yet to be automatically and effectively enforced and implemented by the courts. This implies that even at the present time, a healthy metabolism for state enterprise is still ruled out by political guaranteeism. Money-losing state enterprises (in the PRC or Russia) that should have been declared bankrupt and dissolved are kept alive only by a "blood transfusion" in the form of a government subsidy (denoted by Z_1 and shown as part of the expenditures of the Ministry of Finance in the government finance circle at the top center of figure 1). The monthly paychecks received by the workers of subsidized state enterprises are perpetual unemployment compensation in disguise. The political guarantee of nonbankruptcy of state enterprises is traced directly to the guarantee of "full employment"—an essential component in the welfare package that is politically granted to the urban labor class.

What went wrong with the centrally planned socialistic system (before 1978) can be traced directly to the Marxian ideology that inspired the socialistic experiment, which is the topic we will analyze in the next section. The purpose of this analysis is not so much to gloat in delight at the disintegration of Marxism as it is to search for guiding principles for reform in the years ahead.

III. The Closing of the Case of Karl Marx

The failure of the socialistic experiments—in regard to both the modernization of the agricultural sector and the conduciveness to the requirement of a healthy metabolism—is attributable to the unwarranted faith in Marx's theory. Developed in the 19th century, Marx's theory is quite insensitive to the major critical issues of modern societies in the 20th century. Modernization of the agricultural sector and structural flexibility will be analyzed separately in this section.

3.1 Transition to Modern Economic Growth and Irrelevance of Marxian Ideology

With the arrival of modern economic growth, a modern-growth theorist would draw a rather sharp distinction between short-run transition growth and long-run epochal growth.[8] Furthermore, in the analysis of transition growth, modern economics—making use of a dualistic framework of reasoning (that is, a framework that postulates the coexistence of agricultural and nonagricultural production sectors)—stresses the notion of historical mission that must be played by the agricultural sector for a successful transition into the modern epoch.

The combined history of all socialistic experiments suggests that the central command system is particularly unsuitable for the rural sector. The rural population is less susceptible to the centralism of political command due to the very fact that the population is dispersedly located. In the case of the PRC, the socialistic transformation process was much more stubbornly resisted in the collectivization of the communes than in the nationalization of firms in the urban sector. Total economic reform after 1978 was carried first in the rural sector for the same reason. The agricultural shortfall has always been a critical issue for all ex-socialistic countries. Indeed, there is as yet a single country that has been able to complete the transition growth process and evolve into the epoch of modern growth through socialism.

The general failure of socialistic countries to modernize their agricultural sector is traced partially to the fact that while the socialistic revolution was inspired by Marx, his theory, which is directed at the long-run growth prospect of matured capitalism, is of no use whatsoever to contemporary LDCs that must first modernize the agricultural sector *before* the Marxian theory can be applied at all. Even if the Marxian theory is completely right (which is far from being the case), it is, at best, irrelevant to contemporary lesser-developed countries. The reformers in the PRC finally realize the case of "mistaken identity" by acknowledging that China is now only in the preliminary stages of socialism. Market-oriented reforms must take place in spite of the fact that a glorification of market and prices is certainly counterrevolutionary to Marxian fundamentalists. The need for marketization is particularly strong in the modernization of the agricultural sector—an issue that has puzzled many contemporary growth theorists in the second half of the 20th century, just as it had eluded the Marxian theory of revolution in the middle of the 19th century.

3.2 The Marxian View of Capitalistic Growth in the 19th Century

If the theory of Marx is irrelevant to socialism's failure to modernize the rural sector, his teaching is directly responsible for the failure to modernize the urban sector. This is due to the fact that the organizational features essential for the structural flexibility of "modern" capitalism in the 20th century are far more complicated than that of the 19th century with which Marx was familiar. Let us first examine the Marxian view.

Many of Marx's views on the mode of operation and his sensitivity to social economic problems of capitalism of the 19th century were inherited from the classical writers (Smith, Malthus, Ricardo, 1775-1820) at a time when the transition from agrarianism to EMG in England had just barely begun. The holistic operational perspective of the economic system envisioned by Marx (see figure 2a) is based on a slight modification of the classical system—as succinctly summarized in the numbered boxes (B1, B2, . . ., B7) that will guide our discussion.

Marx envisioned a joint input production process ($Q = f(K, L, t)$ involving the use of capital (K) and labor (L) where the adverse (productivity depressing) effects of the laws of diminishing returns to capital was compensated for only adequately by the intensity of innovation and technology change (box 1 or B1). Like the classical economists before him, Marx had no idea of the virtually unlimited potential of science and technology (for example, computers, space travel, atomic energy, super-conductivity, genetic engineering) that have provided the engine for continuous growth in the 20th century, especially during the second industrial revolution after 1950.

The joint input (K and L) led to the Marxian notion of a class-oriented stratification of families (also inherited from the classical economists) into the capital-owning capitalistic class and the

34

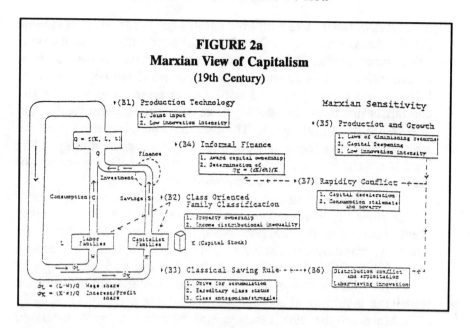

FIGURE 2a
Marxian View of Capitalism
(19th Century)

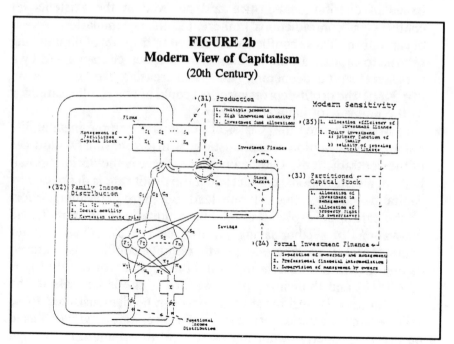

FIGURE 2b
Modern View of Capitalism
(20th Century)

propertyless labor class with implications for the fairness of income distributional justice (box 2). Marx inherited the classical saving rules, according to which the wage income share (ϕ_L) is used for consumption (C) while the property income share (ϕ_K), including interest and profit that need not be differentiated, is used by the capitalists in their insatiable drive for the accumulation and possession of capital assets. The fact that the labor class does not save implies that there can be no interclass social mobility. The hereditary rigidity of the class status constituted the foundation of class antagonism, hatred, and class struggle (box 3).

The "informal" financial institutions were undeveloped, for it serves only the modest purpose of assigning the title to newly created capital wealth (corresponding to investment I) to the saving (that is, capitalistic) families. The growth rate of capital ($\eta_K = (dK/dt)/K$), determined for the economy as a whole, can be identified with the rate of asset accumulation of the capitalistic class under the institutional arrangement of private property (box 4).

Marx, in the 19th century, was sensitive to growth-related issues of distributional justice and believed in the existence of conflicts (or "contradictions") inherent in the accumulation process of capitalism. These conflicts were traced to the laws of diminishing returns to capital. In the modern growth epoch characterized by a persistent capital deepening (that is, increasing capital per head $k = K/L$), the profit-depressing effect could not be compensated for by the intensity of innovations (box 5).

Marx inherited the "Classical Pessimism" (on the inevitability of long-run stagnation of capitalistic growth) by sensing two sources of the contradictions. On the one hand, there is the decided possibility of a distributional conflict when the profit rate is depressed by capital deepening. This will only lead to a more determined effort on the part of the capitalists for labor exploitation (for example, via innovations of a labor-saving variety; see box 6). On the other hand, there is an inherent growth rapidity conflict, as matured capitalism will not be able to sustain the capital growth rate ($\eta_K = d_{\eta K}/dt < 0$) and the consumption welfare of the labor class in the long run (box 7). All these arguments can be demonstrated to be valid with mathematical precision. Hence capitalistic growth based on private property ownership must yield to communism through socialism. The socialistic experiment in the 20th century was inspired by little else beyond this thesis of "scientific" socialism, which was an unconditional prediction of Marx.

Logically, there is nothing wrong with the Marxian theory. What went wrong with the Marxian prediction is that Marx, like the "pessimistic" classical economist before him, failed to see that after the arrival of the modern epoch, the creative potential of the human race in the arena of science and technology is virtually unlimited. Although Marx was quite aware of a "dialectic materialism"—on the relatedness of technology change and the superstructure of the mode of social, political, economic organization—he utterly failed in the application of his own theory of evolution to appreciate the fact that capitalism, as evolved through time, became vastly more complicated (as a result of the development of the various institutions) to accommodate the requirement of structural flexibility in the 20th century.

In addition, Marx failed to foresee how accommodative the "capitalist" class can be toward the various social ills that Marx predicted would make class struggle inevitable. By this, we mean the continuous improvement in pay structure, working conditions, and fringe benefits, not to mention the philanthropies of the capitalists and the various social welfare programs. Of course, one can raise the question of whether the Western world would have been so accommodative if there were no challenges or threats that were originated by the Marxian ideology.

3.3 Capitalism in the 20th Century

The organizational features of modern capitalism in the 20th century are succinctly summarized in figure 2b. Some of these features may have eluded Marx in his design of a blueprint for socialistic experiments (for example, in the *Communist Manifesto*) in the 19th century. As will be pointed out in the last section of this paper, while the Marxian thesis inspired the socialistic experiment, the features that Marx failed to appreciate constituted the focal point of economic reform in all ex-socialistic countries.

The operational perspective of modern (20th century) capitalism contains certain key features as highlighted by boxes 1-5 in figure 2b. There is a morphological resemblance to the Marxian version in figure 2a. What is to be emphasized in this contrast, however, is that as a result of evolution, the modern system (figure 2b) is not only vastly more complicated but is also sensitive to a different set of issues than the class-oriented distributional equity of Marx (figure 2a).

On the production front (box 1), the multiplicity of products and firms (f_i, i = 1, 2, . . .), which is the direct result of innovative creativity, has led to the new organizational task of allocating investment funds (I_i, i = 1, 2, . . .). The problem of income distribution equity becomes more complex, as the issue of functional income distribution (the division into wage and property income) is now separated from the distribution of family income (Y_i, i = 1, 2, . . .) to families (F_i, i = 1, 2, . . .). Marx's class distinction was obliterated as the income of every family (Y_i) is formed of a wage component (w_i) as well as a property income component (π_i). The Keynesian saving rule (box 2) replaced the classical (class-oriented) saving rule because every family can consume (c_i) and save (s_i). If the cultural values of the workers were ever dominated by a preference for class struggle and revolution in the 19th century, the contemporary model is more aptly described by envy, jealously, and a propensity to emulate by exploiting the opportunity for self-reliance.

A key character of modern capitalism is the partitioning of the capital stock from both the management and the ownership standpoint. In the former, the capital stock is partitioned (K_i, i = 1, 2, . . .) to be managed separately by the investment firms (f_i) that are accountable for their managerial outcomes centered in protecting the returns to capital. In the latter, the ownership of capital is partitioned into monetized property rights that are owned by the individual families (F_i) that are not only entitled to the sharing of property income (P_i) but also have the prerogative and incentive to supervise the management (of the partitioned capital stock) in the capacity as the shareholders of the individual firms (box 3).

The management of the capital stock (by the firms, f_i) is, moreover, separated from the ownership (by the families, F_i) via a set of formal financial institutions (for example, banks and stock and bond markets) to professionalize the task of financial inter-mediation and to accommodate the need of asset-owning families for the supervision of management to an extent determined by their own preferred mixture of interests and profit income (box 4). The asset-owning families supervised the management with meticulous care because the value of these assets reflects one's affluence, social status, and perhaps implies political influence and favoritism that the leftists tended to exaggerate.

The separation of ownership and management of the partitioned capital stock is a key characteristic that formed the foundation of structural flexibility for modern capitalism. It is also an institutional innovation that lies behind the drive for CER (see section V).

3.4 Healthy Metabolism of Modern Capitalism

The socialistic experiments in the 20th century were aimed at the construction of an economic institution conceived of and constructed by man via reasoning, blueprint, and design. In sharp contrast, the modern capitalistic system, with all its complexities as we have just described, was the result of an evolutionary outcome that ensures the flexibility of the structure of capital stock (K_1, K_2, . . ., K_n) by a healthy metabolism (i.e., timely birth and death) of the individual firms (f_1, f_2, . . ., f_n). The demand for this flexibility is more profound in the 20th century as compared to the 19th century.

In a modern capitalistic society, this structural flexibility is grounded on two key institutional arrangements oriented toward allocation efficiency:

1. The interest rate that serves to screen alternative investment projects (I_1, I_2, . . ., I_n) that augmented the capital stock (K_1, K_2, . . ., K_n).

2. A culture of (court-enforced) capitalistic legality that supports the formation (via incorporation) and dis-solution (via bankruptcy) of the capitalistic firms (f_1, f_2, . . ., f_n) as the result of a voluntary contract agreement between

39

(a) the asset-owning families (F_i) as owners (e.g., shareholders)

(b) the management and the workers as employees.

Let us discuss the two arrangements respectively. In regard to the screening role of the interest culture, it should be noted that in Marx's aggregate (i.e., single production sector) model (figure 2a), the interest rate and the profit rate need not be differentiated, as they can be (and indeed were) lumped together as property income in the class-oriented distribution analysis (box 2 in figure 2a). This is due primarily to the fact, in the one sector model of Marx, that the significance of interest rate and profit is limited to growth, and distribution as the organizational issue of allocation efficiency is ruled out by definition.

In sharp contrast, modern capitalistic society is extremely sensitive to the issues of both allocation efficiency and family-(rather than class) oriented income distributional equity. For this reason, *a sharp distinction must be drawn between the role of interest and profit.* The interest rate is an objective criterion according to which the future earning potentials of capital stock (K_i) and investment projects (I_i) will be evaluated, assessed, and screened, so that the total investment fund can be allocated rationally. The profits (or loss) are the excess earnings that are accruable primarily to innovation activities in the modern epoch.[9] Without the institutions of interest and profit, investment funds could not be rationally allocated to be accommodative to the requirement of structural flexibility for a modern capitalistic society characterized by the dynamics of science and technology. The revival of an interest culture is an essential prerequisite for successful urban reform in the PRC.

That a capitalistic firm is a voluntary contractual association—that is, assuming an independent legal existence protected by laws—is another institutional arrangement without which the requirement of a healthy metabolism could not be imagined for capitalism. This capitalistic legality defines the contour of a governmental-societal relation in which the role of the government is reduced to protecting the private property right and enforcing contracts. Marx was quite right in viewing the capitalistic legality as a part of the superstructure that accommodated the requirements for the materialism of production. What he failed to see is that at the *heart of the materialism is a healthy metabolism!* It is thus not difficult to see why legal reform is a crucial facet of the CER.

What Marx failed to foresee is that a firm, with its existence threatened by the dynamics of technology, has the "holy right" to fire workers who, except for a brief period of unemployment benefit, must live with a cultural value of self-reliance and take care of their own destiny. Politically guaranteed full employment is thus incompatible with the requirement of structural flexibility in capitalism or socialism. In modern capitalism, all social classes—including labor with its perpetually threatened "social security"—can and must save for the rainy days (that is, to amass a family fortune) as a first line of defense against unemployment. The PRC reformers are only beginning to appreciate this vital lesson and reform their economy accordingly (see the last section).

In summary, the separation of ownership and management of partitioned capital stock, the interest rate, and the independence of the legal existence of the firms are the foundation of the healthy metabolism of modern capitalism. They constitute the guiding principles of CER because these features were insufficiently appreciated by Marx.

IV. Accomplishment and Prospect of Rural Reform

The analysis in the last section is related to urban reform, which will be discussed in section V. We shall, in this section, provide a summary review of rural reform. What has been accomplished in the PRC with respect to agricultural modernization can be described succinctly with the aid of the numbered boxes in figure 1 (B_1, B_2, . . .) that identify the rural reform measures in a holistic operational perspective. As we explained earlier, the purpose of rural reform is to modernize the agricultural sector through the promotion of a mode of urban-rural interaction, characterized by the voluntaristic of decision and the coordination by market forces. For rural reform, we shall discuss three issues: the reform measures, the characteristic of the PRC's reform, and its prospects in the years ahead.

4.1 Rural Reform Measures

The rural reform in the PRC centered on production reorganization and exchange reorganization:

a)   production organization reform aiming at the dissolution of the collectivism of communes and the restoration of family farms (R1);

b)   restoration of the spatially dispersed intersectoral market that accommodated the urban rural exchange (R2).

The rural reform of the PRC is characterized by gradualism in regard to channelization of agricultural surplus, political guaranteeism for consumption, management of the terms of trade, and institution of subsidy:

c)   the channelization of the agricultural surplus was carried out in the two-tract system (R5) representing a hybrid combination of

    i)   retention of compulsory acquisition of agricultural surplus at official prices by state trading, and

    ii)   encouragement of free-market disposal of above quota output conducive to direct urban-rural interactions and contacts;

d)   the relaxation of political guaranteeism of consumption for the urban working class to be replaced by free-market choice (R6);

e)   the gradual removal of the pro-urban bias by the granting of more favorable terms of trade to the farmers in the official tract (R7b);

f)   the institution of a subsidy program to the urban consumers to lessen the adverse impact of improved terms of trade (for farmers) on the urban consumer (R7a).

4.2 Characteristics of Chinese Rural Reform

Rural economic reform has been a unique experience of the de-socialistic evolution in Chinese history, aiming at the construction of a new marketized institution to accommodate urban-rural interaction to complete the transition growth process toward modernization. The evolution was characterized by a gradualism (see points c through f above) which suggests that the Chinese reformers, in their attempt to raise agricultural productivity, are sensitive to two issues: distributional equity and market sensitivity of economic agents.

First of all, China's reformers are sensitive to issues of income distribution justice in the sense that while promoting a policy that eliminated the pro-urban bias (by granting more favorable terms of trade to farmers), the adverse impact on the urban working class (due to the increase of higher prices of agricultural goods) was ameliorated (via, among other actions, the two-tract system and the subsidy program).[10] Instead of emphasizing democratic political reform, reformers used dictatorial political power to arbitrate the urban-rural conflicts via a compromised political solution, as the political interference of the economic system withdraws gradually.

To illustrate the attempt to correct for 30 years of pro-urban bias via the improvement in the terms of trade or the relative price of agricultural products (P_A) to industrial products (P_I), consider the following statistical data: P_A increased 22.13 percent in 1979, while I_I increased a mere 0.09 percent; between 1978 and 1983, the average annual increases in P_A and P_I were 8.35 percent and 0.9 percent respectively; the annual increase in P_I grew to 3.59 percent (relative to a 7.75 percent average annual growth rate in P_A) between 1984 and 1987. It was not until after 1988 that the industrial price increase accelerated (to 15.21 percent in 1988 and 18.71 percent in 1989), perhaps reflecting the spiral inflation generated by the monetary expansion.[11]

The above pattern in terms of the price level and an even more concrete measure in terms of growth in per capita consumption between the urban and rural population are best illustrated with the aid of graphs. Figure 3a is a graphic description of the statistics given above, while figure 3b compares the growth path

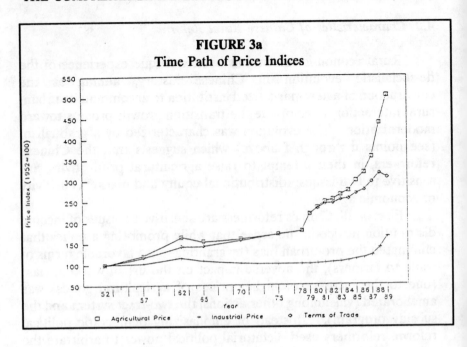

FIGURE 3a
Time Path of Price Indices

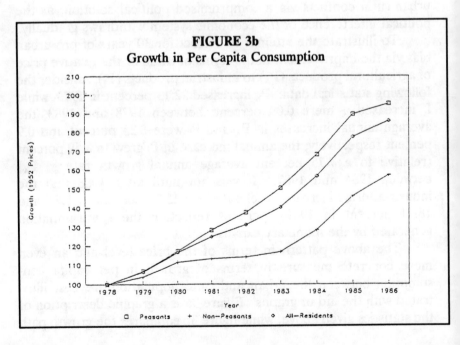

FIGURE 3b
Growth in Per Capita Consumption

of per capita consumption between peasants and nonpeasants. The attempt to correct for the pro-urban bias is indisputable.[12]

The patience of the Chinese reformers can also be seen from the fact that production and exchange reform measures (points a and b above) were carried out before a full liberalization of the market prices was attempted.[13] It would seem that the Chinese approach is safer, because for price reform to be effective, it is obvious that production and exchange reforms are the essential prerequisites to convert the spatially dispersedly located farmers to price (and terms of trade) sensitive economic agents.

Economic reforms in ex-socialistic countries (in China or Russia) will never be successful unless a new class of economic agents (that is, farmers with a modern outlook) can be generated that is responsive to price signals with vitality.[14] The Chinese are fortunate in that they have had a long tradition of family farming and a spatially dispersedly located system of market that can be revived with relative ease—despite their temporary suppression in the period of socialistic transformation (1949-78).

It is perhaps prudent to note that China and Russia, though both attempting to come out of the shadow of the failed socialistic experiment, are very distinct in more than their approach to the transition. It is common knowledge that the Russian reform (at least in the early stages) emphasized political reform over economic rehabilitation, while China's reform is essentially economical with limited political content. The accomplishment differential in terms of economic development, however, is well documented: The phenomenal success of China is a sharp contrast to the near collapse of the Russian economy.

This clearly points to the logical sequence of economic reform preceding political reform, as was the case for China. Nobel Laureate Paul Samuelson (1992) believes that the biggest mistake the U.S.S.R. made was the premature dismissal of central control (totalitarianism) and the bureaucratic system. Extending on this, we believe that a strong central government is perhaps indispensable, at least in the early stages of the transition. Many reform policies are going to be controversial and unpopular, and a central government with a strong will is needed to implement such policies. Furthermore, during the de-socialistic transformation, societal conflicts are inevitable. Urban-rural conflicts, regional frictions, and the competition for resources between industries all need the central government to act as arbitrator.

The difference in performance between China and Russia, however, may go beyond the difference in their emphasis on superficial glasnost/perestroika versus pragmatic economic reform. Two things are definitely in China's favor. First, after only 30 years (1949-78) of socialistic transformation, the capitalist entrepreneur class is still alive. While for Russia, after 70 years, the entrepreneurs are dead (if they were present to begin with). Second, China has had a long cultural tradition (a thousand years or more) of capitalistic farmers who are responsible for their own family welfare by the free disposal of agricultural surplus in exchange with the urban population in the rural markets.[15] In contrast, Russia merely changed from a feudalistic manor system (under the czar) to another "manor" system (under communism). Thus, the interesting question is: Would the Russians have succeeded if they approached reform in the Chinese mode?

4.3 The Completion of the Rural Reform

In the years ahead, the completion of rural reform centers on two issues. The relatively minor issue is the complete withdrawal of the political force from interfering with urban-rural interactions. For this purpose, the atrophy of the subsidy and the compulsory procurement in the official tract are expected to fade away.[16] The major issue is the promotion of interaction between spatially dispersed agricultural and nonagricultural activities—commonly referred to as the township industries—that are currently flourishing in the coastal regions.[17] Specifically we can expect three reform measures to appear:

i)   the promotion of cross-regional labor mobility between agricultural and nonagricultural employment as coordinated by market forces (R10);

ii) the establishment of the financial markets for the rural industries (R4);[18]

iii) land reform (R11) that will be carried out on two fronts:

    a) the privatization of agricultural land to rehabilitate the long traditional Chinese institution that accompanied family farming;

    b) the institutionalization of the separation of land ownership (by the local government) and usage rights (by the township industries) conducive to efficient utilization of nonagriculture land.

All these reforms touch on the ideological issue that will be eroded and revolved in the due course of evolution. Note that the rural reform's focus on the modernization of agriculture is a temporary issue of transition. In contrast, the modernization of industries via the urban reform is a permanent issue that we shall now investigate.

V. Urban Reform: The Rise and Fall of the Socialistic Experiment

Economic reform in a socialistic country is primarily a liberalization process aiming at the establishment of a government-society relation in which the role of the political force will be greatly reduced. Due to the heavier political penetration in the economic system, however, urban reform met with much stiffer resistance from the Communist party, which has vested interests in retaining the power to rule in the party-state. For this reason, reform with regard to large-scale (technological sensitive) state enterprises has barely started.

In our analysis of urban reform in this section, we will limit our discussion to its cause (identified historically from the past, prior to 1978) and its course (projecting into the future, 1992-2010). When we focus our attention on the critical issue of the flexibility of industrial structure, the analysis of the cause and the course is tantamount to a study of the rise and fall of the socialistic experiment—or the opening and the closing of the case of Marx. Our analysis is based on the groundwork of section III, where the features of matured capitalism that support the structural flexibilities have been identified.

5.1 The Rise of Socialism Inspired by the Theory of Marx

The theory of Marx inspired the annihilation of private property during the socialistic transformation period. It follows logically that the urban industries are collectively owned by "all people" (represented by the government) and collectively managed by the bureaucrats (via the centralism of planning and command). Two organizational features follow as a logical consequence:

i)   a meaningful separation of the partitioned capital stock $(K_1, K_2, \ldots, K_n)$ into ownership and management is ruled out by the collectivism of all-people ownership;

ii) the institution of a socialistic state enterprise as a political unit (dedicated to revolution) rather than a voluntary contractual association (dedicated to efficient production and allocation).

Structural rigidity that deprives the socialistic system of a healthy metabolism is the direct result of the teaching of Marx when

i)   the interest rate, as an instrument for the screening of alternative investment projects $(I_1, I_2, \ldots, I_n)$, was abolished as exploitative;

ii) the right of permanent employment of labor as the master class is politically guaranteed.

The destruction of the capitalistic mechanism for structural flexibility by the theory of Marx is complete, though perhaps unintentionally.

5.2 The Fall of the Socialistic Experiment and the Closing of the Case of Marx

The PRC reformers finally recognized that the rigidity of the industrial structure is due to the "nonseparability of enterprise from politics." Our analysis of matured capitalism suggests that in the years ahead, it is absolutely certain that four cardinal convictions will emerge as the guiding principle of urban reform to bring about structural flexibility.

First, the total capital stock should be partitioned $(K_1, K_2, \ldots, K_n)$ to be managed with decentralized responsibility and owned with particularized supervision prerogative. Although portions of the capital stock may be privately or publicly owned, the public-owned portion must be particularized (for example, owned by a town, an army, a ministry, or a school) that will assume the exclusive prerogative of supervision and that presumably will have a strong monetary interest, much like the stockholders of a capitalistic firm. The capital stock can no more be collectively owned than managed. The ownership should be partitioned as the supervisory interests are particularized.

Second, the state enterprises will have to be converted into a voluntary contract association in which the workers can be laid-off permanently in case of bankruptcy. Third, the interest culture must be revived along with flexible market prices as a screening device for investment finance. Fourth, the monetization of all capital assets (that is, the attachment of monetary values to indicate the potential earning power of all partitioned capital stock) is a necessary prerequisite for partitioned ownership.[19]

At the present time, the partition of ownership of capital stock is proceeding in the PRC on two fronts. On the one hand, there is a development of the stock market to attach a monetary value to all capital assets based on a public consensus. On the other hand, there is a movement toward a political partitioning such that each district (province, city, town, and so on) will own and manage their own capital assets with exclusive ownership prerogative and responsibility. China is initiating an experiment, the viability of which will be tested in an evolutionary course in the years ahead. It is, however, virtually certain that with the exception of a few industries characterized by the conspicuous efficiency of large-scale production, the decentralization of the management of partitioned capital stock is the only viable solution in the long run.

As a final note regarding China's population and its severity, it is our firm belief that the labor or employment issue is *the* "beast" that the Chinese reformers need to conquer. The statistics show that between 1978 and 1990, China's population grew by roughly 16 percent. This is not a bad report card and perhaps shows the partial success of the one-child policy. What is devastating is that the labor force grew by close to 40 percent (estimations based on the *China Statistical Abstracts, 1990*).[20]

This is compounded by the fact that there exists vast redundant or surplus labor in both the rural and urban sectors. Conservative estimates indicate that 20 percent of the labor force in state enterprises needs to be laid off if they are to be invigorated.[21] This in and of itself is a significant issue, though perhaps not overwhelming. These factors, combined with the fact that the number of redundant rural workers is expected to swell from 114-152 million, or 30-40 percent (Taylor, 1988) in 1986 to 250 million by the year 2000[22], not to mention the implicit unemployment stemming from the common practice of urban workers retiring at 50 (some as early as 45). These facts intertwine into a maze that will definitely be one of (if not the) nightmares for the reformers.

VI. A Note on China's "Privatization"

As is evident, the increased privatization of the economy under CER (or for that matter, any attempt to transform the centrally planned economy to a market-regulated system) is inevitable. The *getihu* are fast becoming the most economically active class in China. Its growth, both in number and productivity, is extraordinary to say the least. Direct measures, however, are hard to find. Even if one could obtain such data, it is likely to be sketchy, ambiguous, and perhaps understated.

Table 3 presents a rough estimate of the size of private enterprises in industry. The table is derived from Field (1992), where he measures the gross value of industrial output by (among other things) the type of ownership. Column one measures the total industrial output (in 1980 prices), while column two is the output that is all or partially owned by private individuals. Column three is the sum of the industrial output produced from privately owned enterprises, which are further broken down into city and other measurements (county, town) in columns four and five respectively. Column six is the sum of industrial output produced by enterprises that are jointly owned by the public and private individuals. Columns seven and eight subdivide the above by the nature of the joint ownership, individual-state, and individual-collective, respectively.

More important than the absolute size of the output value is its growth rate. In the parentheses that follow each of the columns described below is the corresponding growth rate relative to the previous year. As can be clearly seen, the growth rate of private industrial output is consistently larger—significantly larger, one might add—than that of overall growth. The average annual growth rate of the industrial output is 12.75 percent, while the corresponding rate for private industrial enterprises (column 2) is 158.66 percent.

TABLE 3

Privatization Content in Industrial Production

Year	Industrial Output		Private Industrial Output	
1980	5,230.87		0.86	
1981	5,455.48	(4.29)	2.01	(133.72)
1982	5,882.11	(7.82)	4.17	(107.46)
1983	6,540.60	(11.20)	8.05	(93.05)
1984	7,606.30	(16.29)	19.65	(144.10)
1985	9,255.33	(21.68)	189.58	(864.78)
1986	10,309.54	(11.39)	330.53	(74.35)
1987	12,134.60	(17.70)	528.06	(59.76)
1988	14,658.71	(20.80)	801.56	(51.79)
1989	15,909.90	(8.54)	1,035.42	(29.18)
1990	17,144.51	(7.76)	1,329.73	(28.42)

(Continued on next page)

TABLE 3 (Continued)
Privatization Content in Industrial Production

Year	Total		Individual City		Other	
1980	0.81		0.81		-	
1981	1.88	(132.10)	1.88	(132.10)	-	
1982	3.44	(82.98)	3.44	(82.98)	-	
1983	7.54	(119.19)	7.54	(119.19)	-	
1984	14.81	(96.42)	14.81	(96.42)	-	
1985	179.75	(1113.70)	33.39	(125.46)	146.36	
1986	308.54	(71.65)	29.13	(-12.76)	279.41	(90.91)
1987	483.09	(56.57)	46.26	(58.81)	436.83	(56.34)
1988	712.09	(47.40)	59.03	(27.61)	653.06	(49.50)
1989	881.39	(23.78)	72.25	(22.40)	809.14	(23.90)
1990	1,067.46	(21.11)	-		-	

Year	Total		Joint: Individual- State		Collective	
1980	0.05		-		0.05	
1981	0.13	(160.00)	-		0.13	(160.00)
1982	0.73	(461.53)	0.70		0.03	(-76.92)
1983	0.51	(-30.14)	0.48	(-31.42)	0.03	(0.00)
1984	4.84	(849.02)	4.68	(975.00)	0.16	(433.33)
1985	9.83	(103.10)	8.27	(76.71)	1.56	(875.00)
1986	21.99	(123.70)	18.02	(117.90)	3.97	(154.49)
1987	44.97	(104.50)	35.53	(97.17)	9.44	(137.78)
1988	89.47	(98.96)	68.74	(93.47)	20.73	(119.60)
1989	154.03	(72.16)	107.64	(56.59)	46.39	(123.78)
1990	262.27	(70.27)	180.51	(67.70)	81.76	(76.25)

Notes: All production values are in 100 million yuan and measured in 1980 constant prices. Growth rates (relative to the previous year) are in parentheses.

Source: Adapted from table A3 of Field (1992).

In a more conservative measure, the total industrial output grew at an average annual rate of 13.24 percent during the last five years, while the narrowly defined private industrial enterprises (column 3) grew at 44.10 percent. It is thus clear that the fastest growing sector of privatization is the joint-ownership type of enterprise (as can be seen in table 4 and the accompanying figure 4). With the development of the stock market and the partitioning of the capital stock ownership (section V), the boom in such entrepreneurial structure is perhaps the wave of the future and an intermediate step before the full privatization of the economy.

Two recent cases certainly point toward this trend. First, Guangdong declared (24 February 1993) its intention to accelerate toward a stock/shareholder-owned limited company system.[23] In 1992, Guangdong (excluding Guangzhou and Shenzhen) approved 161 such companies, which total 25.4 billion shares (of which corporate/legal entities account for 87 percent of the shares, while natural persons hold 13 percent). In 1993, Guangdong plans to request the authorization for one-third of the large/medium state enterprises to be converted to mainly corporate (legal) persons owned companies. These will be managed autonomously and will behave as a self-reliant modern enterprise.

A second example is the Sichuan provincial government's announcement (26 February 1993) that it will auction off 16 money-losing state enterprises in Hong Kong between 15-21 April. The form of the transaction can be outright purchase, operation contracts, rental, or partial capital investment. This is an interesting example, as Sichuan is a more inland province.[24] The action is also more direct and more radical. If this proves to be a successful formula, one would certainly expect other provinces to follow suit.

The above paints only part of the bigger picture. It is not complete even for the industrial sector, as the underground economy is hard to gauge. Several studies have placed the size of the underground economy for Taiwan and South Korea to be perhaps one-third of their GNPs. This is not to say that the magnitude is comparable in China, but it is certainly worth keeping in mind when trying to gauge the contribution of private entrepreneurs.

TABLE 4
Private Industrial Output
(as Percentage of Total Industrial Output)

Year	Private	Individual	Joint
1980	0.0164	0.0155	0.0010
1981	0.0368 (124.39)	0.0345 (122.58)	0.0024 (140.00)
1982	0.0709 (92.66)	0.0585 (69.57)	0.0124 (416.67)
1983	0.1231 (73.62)	0.1153 (97.09)	0.0078 (-37.10)
1984	0.2583 (109.83)	0.1947 (68.86)	0.0636 (715.38)
1985	2.0483 (892.99)	1.9421 (897.48)	0.1062 (66.98)
1986	3.2061 (56.52)	2.9928 (54.10)	0.2133 (100.85)
1987	4.3517 (35.73)	3.9811 (33.02)	0.3706 (73.75)
1988	5.4681 (25.65)	4.8578 (22.02)	0.6104 (64.71)
1989	6.5080 (19.02)	5.5399 (14.04)	0.9681 (58.60)
1990	7.7560 (19.18)	6.2262 (12.39)	1.5298 (58.02)

NOTES: Figures derived from Table 3.
Annual growth rate in parentheses.

FIGURE 4
Growth of Private Industrial Enterprise

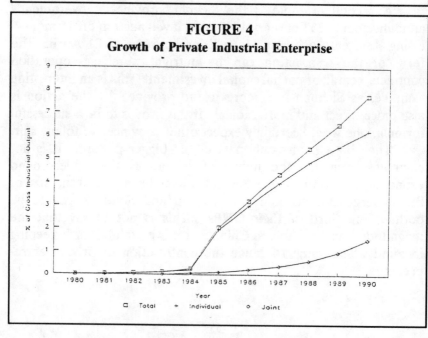

54

The tremendous increase in the free-market track of the agricultural sector is certainly an important aspect. Indeed, the dual-track system in terms of agricultural production was the most important part of China's rural reform and the centerpiece of the first seven years of the CER (Hou, Fei, and Wang, 1993). An often neglected and arguably equally important aspect of privatization, however, is the service sector. In a capitalistic economy, the service and commercial sector is often termed the "fabric" of the economy. The statistics are not directly available, but there is ample evidence of the growth and potential in the privatized service sector.

For example, in its report (see footnote 21), the Economic Research Center of the Textile Ministry recommended that state enterprises, like the textile industry, disperse their surplus labor toward the service sector because:

1. The textile factories have superior geographical location. This creates advantageous conditions for the development of real estate, commerce, financial, and information services.

2. In the current stage of development for the textile industry itself, there is a great need for information, financial, and technological (R&D) services to serve the furthering of the industry.

Though it did not specifically state the nature of these service enterprises, it is perhaps not unreasonable to assume that at least part of them will be private or jointly owned and managed.

Further evidence can be seen in the conversion of the 7,000 state owned and managed commercial retail stores in Beijing into state-owned privately operated enterprises, half of which are already converted, with a completion date expected in October of 1993. These stores include nonstaple food stores, grocery (vegetable) stores, grain stores, and small department or general stores. These were the backbone of the infrastructure that guaranteed food and clothing during the centrally planned days. After the liberalization of the market, the centrally planned and managed stores such as these were not able to compete with the privatized stores and peddlers; thus, such a reform is inevitable.

The operational principle is based on the separation of property ownership and management. It will be state-owned assets, property/equipment rented out, self-reliant on fund/capital raising, privately operated. The objective is to raise the risk resistance ability of the small enterprises and improve the organizational mode, all the while improving economic efficiency. These are the counterparts of the joint state/collective-individual enterprises of the industrial sector discussed previously (and shown in table 3). It is also stated that those small enterprises with a long record of losses or extremely small profits, after approval, can be sold directly to the employees or auctioned off publicly. This would constitute the counterpart of private (city), individually owned enterprises in the industrial sector.

Conclusion

In the long-run, as rural reform is brought to a successful conclusion (that is, as the modernized agricultural sector fulfills its historical mission), the spotlight of CER will eventually shift to urban reform to ensure the utilization of resources with efficiency, which in the 20th century is much more important than Marx realized in the 19th century. Moreover, efficiency is not only a matter of static "Pareto optimality," as emphasized (perhaps overly emphasized) by microeconomic theory. For a healthy metabolism, which is a necessary condition for allocation efficiency, implies other advantages due to the implied diversity through experimental creativity. In his eloquent defense of capitalism at the darkest moment of the depressive 1930s, Keynes (1951) wrote:

> Let us stop for a moment to remind ourselves what these advantages are. They are partly advantages of efficiency—the advantages of decentralization and the play of self-interest. The advantage to efficiency of the decentralization of decisions and of individual responsibility is even greater, perhaps, than the

nineteenth century supposed; and the reaction against the appeal to self-interest may have gone too far. But, above, all, individualism, if it can be purged of its defects and its abuses, is the best safeguard of personal liberty in the sense that, compared with any other system, it greatly widens the field for the exercise of personal choice. It is also the best safeguard of the variety of life, which emerges precisely from this extended field of personal choice, and the loss of which is the greatest of all losses of the homogeneous or totalitarian state. For this variety preserves the tradition which embody the most secure and successful choices of former generations; it colors the present with the diversification of its fancy; and, being the handmaid of experiment as well as tradition and of fancy, it is the most powerful instrument to better the future. (*General Theory*, p. 380).

Thus, the healthy metabolism and structural flexibility that urban reform aims to achieve, besides the narrowly defined advantages of efficiency, is also conducive to a lifestyle characterized by the freedom of creativity and a richness of variety. It is ultimately for these higher transcendental values that the urban reform will go on in the years ahead in China—as well as in other ex-socialistic countries—in search for the meaning of human dignity.

REFERENCES

Ash, Robert F. "The Agricultural Sector in China: Performance and Policy Dilemmas during the 1990s," *China Quarterly* 131 (1992): 545-76.

Decision. "Decision of the Central Committee of the CCP on Reform of the Economic Structure," reprinted (in English) in the *Beijing Review*, 29 October 1984, 27(44).

Fei, John C. H. and Jack W. Hou. 1992a. "Capitalism and Urban Reform in Socialistic PRC," presented at the 34th Annual Conference of the Western Social Science Association, 22-25 April 1992, Denver, Colorado.

Fei, John C. H. and Jack W. Hou. 1992b. "Monetization of the Chinese Economy," presented at the 67th Annual Conference of the Western Economic Association, 9-13 July 1992, San Francisco, California.

Field, Robert Michael. "China's Industrial Performance Since 1978," *China Quarterly* 131 (1992): 577-607.

Hou, Chia-Chu, and Jack W. Hou. "Stages and Policies of Economic Development in Taiwan," presented at the 67th Annual Conference of the Western Economic Association, 9-13 July 1992, San Francisco, California, and the 31st Annual Western Conference of the Association for Asian Studies, 22-24 October 1992, at University of Arizona, Tucson, Arizona.

Hou, Chia-Chu, and Jack W. Hou. 1993. "Trade Liberalization in Taiwan," in Leonard F. S. Wang and Ping-Wen Lin (eds.), *Economic Development, Trade, and Liberalization in Taiwan* (Amsterdam: Kluwer Academic Publishers), forthcoming.

Hou, Jack W., and Jack W. Appleton. 1993. "The 'Engine' of Taiwan's Economic Growth: A Path Analysis Approach," presented at the 35th Annual Conference of the Western Social Science Association 21-24 April 1993, Corpus Christi Texas.

Hou, Jack W., John C. H. Fei, and Yia-Jin Wang. 1993. "Rural Reform: Evolution of the Dualistic Economy of Socialistic China," presented at the 67th Annual Conference of the Western Economic Association, 9-13 July 1992, San Francisco, California, and the 19th Annual Conference of the Eastern Economic Association, 19-21 March 1993, Washington, D.C.

Hou, Jack W., and Kui Wai Li. 1993. "Monetization and the Financial Inter-Relationships in China's Economic Reform," scheduled to be presented at the 68th Annual Conference of the Western Economic Association, 20-24 June 1993, Lake Tahoe, Nevada.

Hou, Jack W., and Intae Myong. 1993. "The Role of the External Sector in China's Economic Reform," presented at the 31st Annual Western Conference of the Association for Asian Studies, 22-24 October 1992, University of Arizona, Tucson, Arizona, and the 19th Annual Conference of the Eastern Economic Association, 19-21 March 1993, Washington, D.C.

Keynes, John Maynard. *The General Theory of Employment, Interest, and Money.* London: Macmillan and Co., 1951. First printed in 1936.

Kuo, Shirley W. Y., Gustav Ranis and John C. H. Fei. *The Taiwan Success Story: Rapid Growth with Improved Distribution in the Republic of China, 1952-1979.* Boulder: Westview Press, 1981.

Kuznets, Simon. *Modern Economic Growth, Rate, Structure, and Spread.* New Haven: Yale University Press, 1966.

Lardy, Nicholas. *Agriculture in China's Modern Economic Development.* Cambridge: Cambridge University Press, 1983.

Li, K. T. *The Evolution of Policy Behind Taiwan's Development Success.* New Haven: Yale University Press, 1988.

Lin, C. Y. *Industrialization in Taiwan 1946-72: Trade and Import Substitution Policies for Developing Countries.* New York: Praeger Publishers, 1973.

Perkins, Dwight Heald. *Agriculture Development in China, 1368-1968.* Chicago: Aldine, 1969.

Samuelson, Paul. A. "China: A Sleeping Economic Giant," *China Times*, 25 May 1992, Taipei, Taiwan.

Sicular, Terry. "Agricultural Planning and Pricing in the Post-Mao Period," *China Quarterly*, 115: 671-705.

Skinner, G. William. "Marketing and Social Structure in Rural China," *Journal of Asian Studies*, 24(1): 3-43 (part I), 24(2):195-228 (part II), 24(1):363-99 (part III).

Taylor, Jeffrey R. "Rural Employment Trends and the Legacy of Surplus Labor, 1978-86," *China Quarterly*, 115:737-66.

Walker, R. "Trends in Crop Production, 1978-86," *China Quarterly*, 115:592-633.

ENDNOTES

1. This "external orientation" is also a prominent characteristic of the CER (Hou and Myoung, 1993). We shall de-emphasize this external orientation aspect, however, to stress an evolutionary perspective that is primarily an internal matter.

2. The PRC reforms stressed the slogan of "four modernizations," which in the final analysis, amounts to "modernization via science and technology."

3. For the case of Taiwan, there exists an abundance of literature. See, for example, Lin (1973), Kuo, Ranis, and Fei (1981), Li (1988), Hou and Hou (1992, 1993), and Hou and Appleton (1993).

4. In this regard, we should add that a liberalization process also started in Taiwan after 1980 as the marketing institutions were strengthened.

5. Technically, there is a third component: reform for external orientation. See Hou and Myoung (1993) for more details.

6. In a historical perspective, the initiation of transition growth in both England and Japan were heralded by an "agriculture revolution" just as much as a "green revolution" is a key ingredient of transition growth for contemporary LDCs.

7. Though in the early stages this was not as severe, it became more serious as CER progressed. For example, during the period 1987-90, China lost approximately 5.67 million hectares of arable land to nonagricultural use, which translates to 37.5 million tons of grain (Sicular, 1988).

8. See the discussion on the "Historical Perspective" in Section I above.

9. In the language of economists, "interest" is an equilibrium concept, while "profit" is a disequilibrium concept.

10. For example, the cereals subsidy in 1981 reached 12.9 billion yuan, or 10 percent of total government expenditure (Lardy, 1983). In a broader context, the state price subsidy for grain, oil crops, and cotton grew from 12 million yuan in 1980 to 16.3 million in 1981 and to 17 million in 1982. In terms of the proportion of the state budget, this translates to an increase from 10 percent of total government expenditure in 1980 to 15 percent in 1982. See Sicular (1988) for more details.

11. This, combined with the coming of age of rural reform in terms of agricultural production, has presented a new crisis. The continued increase in the productivity of the agricultural sector has lowered the free-market price. At the same time, the government's retreat in terms of subsidies has lowered procurement prices and raised retail prices (refer to Hou, Fei, and Wang, 1993, for a more detailed theoretical model). Thus, the farmers are producing more food than ever, yet their income did not increase. The Chinese government has repeatedly expressed its concern and commitment to the improvement of the livelihood of farmers.

12. An alternative perspective is to examine the "orientation of development strategy" (ODS). Prior to CER (1978-), the socialistic ODS was in the order of heavy industry, light industry, agriculture. This can be clearly seen in the output indices (1983): base year 1952 (or $Index_{1952} = 100$)

2571 (Heavy) > (Light) > 336 (Agriculture)

After CER, a light industry orientation was pursued emphasizing consumption orientation and agriculture (fertilizer) orientation. This historical pattern can be clearly seen in the average annual growth rate by periods:

	1952–57	1957–66	1966–78	1978–84
Heavy industry	22.7	10.9	10.1	5.0
Light industry	12.1	8.5	7.5	10.6
Agriculture	4.4	2.0	3.6	7.6

13. In sharp contrast, the Russian rural reform in January 1992 began with a full floating of the prices of the agriculture goods—raising them by over 750 percent—without the benefits of reform in production and/or exchange reorganization.

14. An extension of this entrepreneur peasant class is the farmer turned "specialized" households. These form the backbone of China's booming township enterprises, which are accounting for more than 40 percent of total industrial production and rising.

15. Perkins (1969) and Skinner (1974).

16. For example, the ratio of free-market price to contract procurement price for the rice and wheat (in selected years) were:

	1978	1980	1982	1984
Rice	2.31	1.57	1.57	1.00
Wheat	2.10	1.30	1.21	1.00

Refer to Sicular (1988) for more details.

17. In employment terms, between 1985 and 1989, the number of workers employed by the state enterprises increased by a total of 12.44 percent, as compared to the 34.21 percent registered by the township enterprises (*China Facts and Figures Annual*, 1990).

18. As discussed earlier, the lack of a proper profit-seeking and interest rate regulated financial market is at the roots of the structural rigidity of the Marxian system. An often neglected aspect of the CER is the "monetization" (that is, the

reemergence of the monetary culture) of the economy, which is a prerequisite for the development of a modern financial market (Fei and Hou, 1992b; Hou and Li, 1993).

19. For a more detailed discussion of the theoretical fundamentals that plague the socialistic economic structure, refer to Fei and Hou (1992ab).

20. This, of course, is the residual of Mao's legacy of encouraging population growth (that is, those that were born during the Cultural Revolution era are entering the labor force).

21. For example, in February of 1993, the Economic Research Center of the Textile Ministry estimates that more than 30 percent of the 7.5 million workers employed in the state enterprises in the textile industry is redundant and suggests dispersing them (within the next four years) mainly to the service sector.

22. Based on 1988 reports on rural development by the State Council's Rural Development Center and the Rural Development Institute of the Chinese Academy of Social Sciences.

23. The "stockholders" or shareholders are predominantly corporate (legal) persons/entities rather than natural persons.

24. Sichuan is nevertheless extremely enthusiastic and active in the reform process. In fact, it spearheaded many of the programs, since Zhao Ziyang's rise was mainly due to his success in managing the economic development of Sichuan that later became the economic model for all of China.

CHAPTER THREE

Chinese Society Under Deng

DEBORAH S. DAVIS

The reforms of Deng Xiaoping have materially transformed Chinese society. New high-rise apartment buildings, television towers, and microwave transmitters crowd city skylines. Advertisements for Sony, Siemans, Pepsi, and Coke compete for attention at intersections where billboards previously had warned against intrusions by the dangerous bourgeoisie. The extensive fields of the People's Communes have been subdivided into a patchwork of small family farms, and commune centers, which previously focused on the activities of the Communist party, are dominated by the bustle of daily markets and extensive trade with rural industries.

At the same time, however, as the Deng economic reform has dramatically altered China's physical landscape, many Maoist institutions and ideological priorities continue to shape Chinese society. The massacre in Tiananmen brutally reminded outside observers how committed and unyielding Deng and his colleagues could be to any who overtly challenged their political monopolies. It also revealed how divided and contentious Chinese society had become when caught between an unfinished revolution and partial reform.

Since 1990, the CCP leadership has been reconfigured and structural economic reforms once more encourage competitive markets for land, labor, and capital. Yet key monopolies in banking, finance, and commerce remain, and industrial reforms are constrained by quotas and administrative prices. Structural reform continues to be a priority, but social changes proceed in a somewhat lurching pattern where compromise rather than hard rejection of China's socialist past dominates.

To illustrate how crosscurrents of change and continuity animate contemporary Chinese society, this essay examines several social policy arenas where the Deng leadership initiated radical departures from Maoist practice, but where actual implementation has led to unexpected continuity as well as change. Social policies are often treated as a secondary tier of government action that does not require the same scrutiny as economic, political, or diplomatic programs. Because it is precisely policies in these spheres, however, that mold the human resources which ultimately determine a society's future, discussion of such issues as population control, migration, retirement, and education complements analysis of the political economy as well as the more circumscribed sphere of social welfare.

Changes in Population Policies

In December 1978 the Chinese population of 962 million was the largest in the world. It was also overwhelmingly agricultural, with more than 80 percent of the population living in one of China's five million villages and hamlets.[1] Despite these huge numbers, however, by the late 1970s the annual rate of population growth appeared to have stabilized at an annual rate of 1.2 percent[2] (see Table 1). Therefore, China occupied a demographically anomalistic position. In terms of economic structure and per capita wealth, its peers were India, Indonesia, and Nigeria, but in terms of fertility and population growth, it more closely resembled the nations of Europe or North America than those of Asia and Africa.[3]

China also differed from virtually all other large agrarian nations in the severe and effective controls the central government imposed on population movements within the nation. After nearly 25 years of industrial growth, the percentage of citizens living in the countryside (*xiangcun*) had only declined from 87 percent in 1952 and to 82 percent in 1977.[4] City residence and the comforts of urban living remained a privilege reserved for a small minority while the vast majority of adults remained in the countryside throughout their entire lives.

TABLE 1
Demographic Trends

Year	CBR	CDR	TFR Total	TFR Rural	TFR Urban	NGR	Total Population
1952	37.0	17.0	6.47	-	-	16.0	574m
1957	34.0	10.8	6.40	-	-	23.2	646m
1964	39.1	11.5	6.17	-	-	27.6	704m
1970	33.4	7.6	5.81	6.38	3.27	25.8	829m
1978	18.2	6.2	2.72	2.97	1.55	12.0	962m
1979	17.8	6.2	2.75	3.05	1.37	11.6	975m
1980	18.2	6.3	2.24	2.48	1.15	11.8	987m
1981	20.9	6.3	2.63	2.91	1.39	14.5	1.000b
1982	22.2	6.6	2.65	-	1.73	15.6	1.016b
1983	20.1	6.9	2.08	-	1.61	13.2	1.030b
1984	19.9	6.8	2.03	-	1.46	13.0	1.043b
1985	21.0	6.7	2.04	-	1.23	14.2	1.058b
1986	22.4	6.8	2.44	-	1.43	15.5	1.075b
1987	23.3	6.7	2.84	-	1.38	16.6	1.093b
1988	22.3	6.6	-	-	-	15.7	1.110b
1989	21.5	6.6	-	-	-	15.0	1.127b
1990	21.0	6.6	2.25	2.70	1.40	14.3	1.143b

CBR: crude birth rate   **CDR:** crude death rate
TFR: total fertility rate   **NGR:** natural growth rate

Sources: for CBR, CDR, NGR, and total population, *Zhongguo tongji nianjian 1991* (hereafter *ZGTJNJ 1991*) (Beijing: Zhongguotongji chubanshe, 1991), 79–80; for 1952–1964 TFRs, Judith Banister, *China's Changing Population* (Stanford: Stanford University Press, 1987, 230; for 1970–1987 TFRs, Susan Greenhalgh, "Socialism and Fertility in China," *Annals, AAPSS*, no. 510 (July 1990), 73–86; for 1990 TFR, *ZGTJNJ 1991*, 90 and *Renmin ribao* (hereafter *RMRB*) 18 December 1990, 4.

In 1980 CCP population policies—both as they related to fertility rates and domestic migration—changed significantly. Despite trends that had made China the envy of the third world, Deng reformers found that even if the population only grew at 1.2 percent per year, by the middle of the 21st century it would reach two billion. In response to such projections, the Deng planners set a "population ceiling" of 1.2 billion for the year 2000 and a long-term goal of a stable population of under 900 million by the end of the 21st century.[5] To achieve such radical and ambitious demographic targets, they drafted the equally radical and ambitious policy goal of a nationwide birth quota of one child per woman.

The impressive fertility declines after 1970 had been the result of many different factors. Officially the key was a national policy that advocated "later marriage, longer spacing between births, and fewer children." In fact, birth rates plummeted because of several different social policies initiated during the 1950s that had improved survival rates among children, reduced female illiteracy, increased the labor power of mothers, and raised the cost of child rearing. Initial public health programs that improved hygiene and curbed the spread of the most lethal infectious diseases greatly reduced child mortality, while investment in basic education and a policy of full employment for women as well as men made young mothers active participants in the labor force. As a result, in the early 1970s the majority of new brides entered their childbearing years expecting to work outside the home, expecting their infants to survive to adulthood, and educationally prepared to practice effective contraception. During the Cultural Revolution, additional efforts to delay first marriages (and therefore first births) slowed total population growth further by delaying entry of the 1950s baby boom into motherhood, but it was the basic investments in public health and education as well as advances in cheap contraceptive technologies that allowed Chinese young women during the 1970s to control fertility more effectively than any previous generation.

The one-child policy launched in 1979 therefore marked a radical departure from past practices. Instead of a multifaceted approach that relied primarily on voluntary compliance and indirect incentives and did not demand a single modal family size, the initial policy for the one-child campaign was compulsory, uniform, and rigid. Subsequently, the restrictions were relaxed for rural couples whose first child was a girl or who could claim a singleton would impose economic hardship. As a result, fertility rates quickly rose and by 1990 both the crude birth rate (CBR) and natural growth rate (NGR) exceeded those of 1978 (see Table 1).

In terms of outcomes other than CBR and NGR, however, the one-child campaign has had a significant, if unplanned, impact. Although the aggregate fertility measures did not decline after 1980, parity rates did. After 1980 approximately 90 percent of all city births have been first births and in rural areas there has been a dramatic decline in the percentage of fourth or higher order births.[6] Although such shifts do not immediately create fundamental social change, in the long term they could widen the gap between rural and urban family life.

With the vast majority of young urban families now raising only one child, the urban family structure has been revolutionized. Achieving completed family size within two or three years of marriage, urban family life is by necessity not as focused on parental roles as it was when childbearing continued over 10 or 12 years of marriage. As a result, young urban couples are likely to develop attitudes toward marital sexuality that differ significantly from older couples whose marriages focused on procreation and whose household contained more children than parents.

With over 90 percent of urban births after 1980 first-births, the newest generation of urban families also experiences other aspects of everyday life in a distinctive fashion. As of 1992, few city primary schools include any siblings. Each parent whom a teacher sees is a parent of an only child, and almost no parent has any point of reference other than their singleton. When these young families look for housing it is for a family of three, not one that will expand to four or five. These urban families of two parents and one child also anticipate an old age radically different than that of earlier generations. If the one-child norm continues for another 25 years, the typical urban family will consist of four grandparents, two parents, and one grandchild. Except among the oldest generations, there will be no aunts, uncles, cousins, nephews, or nieces.

By contrast, in the rural areas, where young couples in their 30s almost never have a singleton and the government appears to have abandoned the one-child ideal, family life is very different. Siblings are the norm in the family and in the schools. Sexual relations focus on procreation, and marital roles can be subordinated to parental obligations. Planning for old age continues to be focused on intergenerational "contracts" whereby children are obliged to support parents in return for the support parents gave earlier. During the Mao era, urban and rural families also differed. With the emergence of a modal one-child family in cities, however, the distinctions became starker and the distance between rural and urban family expectations widened.

The second Deng population policy to shape Chinese society is in the area of migration controls.[7] Throughout most of the Mao era, CCP leadership pursued a policy to limit the size of the urban population, and to achieve this goal they imposed both economic and administrative restrictions on movement between the cities and the countryside. At the core was a state grain policy that restricted subsidized grain sales to the nonagricultural residents of towns and cities. Suburban and village residents were prohibited from either buying subsidized grain or selling grain in open markets. In this way, rural residents were immobilized by a migration policy that effectively tethered rural men to the villages of their birth and rural women to the villages of their husbands.

Within just a few years of launching the Four Modernizations, the Deng reformers had either dismantled or seriously compromised these Maoist constraints on rural to urban migration. At first the changes were modest amendments to existing regulations to permit reunification of family members long separated by work assignments or to legalize the temporary residence of entrepreneurial rural sojourners.[8] By the mid-1980s, however, there were fundamental reforms. Sales of grain became less restricted, and 60,000 market towns were permitted to accept any rural newcomer who started a new business or found long-term employment.[9] By the late 1980s, rural residents of peri-urban areas moved unimpeded between their suburban homes and the urban core. Millions of others came daily as traders, haulers, and construction laborers and also as investors and consumers in the urban economy. They participated in credit associations, established homes, and frequented the restaurants and discos of the newly expanded night life. By December 1988, more than 46 million rural migrants had acquired formal urban registration,[10] and millions more had quit village life and become *de facto* urban residents.[11] Two years later, the government announced that there were 70 million migrant workers;[12] unofficial Hong Kong observers estimated the total to be closer to 100 million.[13] In some cities in the rapidly developing southern frontier, officials reported that up to 25 percent of the population now came from outside the surrounding countries, and in the large metropolitan areas of Shanghai, Beijing, and Guangzhou, more than one million outsiders participated in the urban economy on a daily basis.[14]

A surge toward the cities was not unprecedented. During the 1950s, migration out of the countryside also swelled urban centers. British economist Christopher Howe estimates that during the first Five Year Plan, rural to urban migration accounted for 33.6 percent of the population growth in Shanghai, 43 percent in Guangzhou, and an astounding 70 percent in Beijing.[15] Then, as in the 1980s, rural migrants came to escape poverty and accept jobs that the resident urbanites would not or could not perform. During the 1950s, however, out-migration from villages occurred at the same time that millions of urban intellectuals and technicians were being relocated outside the cities either as a result of political *xia fang* campaigns or as part of a redeployment of technical experts to the underdeveloped interior.[16]

The migration of the 1950s also differed from that of the 1980s in terms of its relationship to commerce and entrepreneurship. During the 1950s, rural migrants flowed to jobs in industry, and urban out-migrants went to the interior to construct factories, build dams, and staff new technical schools. The migration of the 1980s, by contrast, has been driven by trade and petty capitalism. At the height of the migration in 1957, peddling was a furtive strategy of survival; in 1992 it is often the first hopeful step onto the ladder of entrepreneurial success. Because commerce and individual salesmanship are now at the heart of these vast movements between village and city, the demographic flux of the 1980s has not only created busier, more crowded urban markets, it also has laid the foundations for a new social hierarchy. When rural peddlers earn more than state workers and when the ambitious see no gain from joining the communist bureaucracy, core principles of the Maoist social order have been eclipsed. Therefore, although the vast majority of Chinese citizens remain in small rural villages and permanent moves to the cities continue to be difficult, there have been fundamental ideological and behavioral shifts that create the potential for additional structural changes over the next decade.

Changes in Welfare Policies

In the welfare area, the Deng reformers have often spoken in a rhetoric of commodification that, if fully implemented, would have dramatically altered programs for the old, disabled, and dependent. As in the case of the one-child policy, reality and rhetoric diverged, however, and significant unplanned shifts resulted.

At the end of the Mao era Chinese social welfare standards were impressive. Basic medical services reached the majority of citizens and most of the frail and disabled received subsistence. In rural areas, village cooperatives and user-fees funded direct services and central government expenditures provided public health, famine relief, and hospital construction. In the cities, workplace and neighborhood associations provided a complete range of welfare services. All state employees qualified for free medical care and pensions, workers in the collective sector received medical subsidies and lump sum pensions, and low-rent public housing was the norm for all urbanites.[17]

In rural areas, the demise of the commune and the return of family farming after 1980 appeared to threaten the community support for village welfare programs, while in urban areas refutation of Maoism and advocacy of competition and commodification contradicted the core ideological justification of earlier commitments. After more than a decade of explicit retreat from the Maoist model, however, Deng welfare reforms have simultaneously provided unexpected continuity in some areas while creating preconditions for further change in others. A brief discussion of pension policy and outcomes during the 1980s illustrates this phenomenon.

Urban workers were first offered old age pensions in 1951, but because workers needed 20 years of work experience in a participating enterprise to qualify, it was only when the first cohorts of post-1949 state employees entered their 50s and 60s during the late 1960s and early 1970s that pensions became a major benefit. Because that chronological turning point coincided with a radical phase of the Cultural Revolution when union officials came under attack as hidden bourgeoisie and welfare perquisites were denigrated as antisocialist, however, there was neither organizational nor ideological support for a massive pension program. Therefore, the demise of the Gang of Four in 1976 and repudiation of the most "leftist" policies of the 1970s would undoubtedly have initiated a sudden upsurge in the number of pensioners, yet the growth of the 1980s was also the creation of specific Deng policy shifts.[18]

First the retirement regulations were amended in 1978 to reduce work requirements and improve the benefits. Second, enterprise managers were encouraged to make retirement mandatory, and third, every new retiree was promised that they could select any one of their adult children not already employed in an urban state job to replace (*dingti*) them in their unit. Workers in their 60s who had been delaying retirement for financial reasons and parents whose children were languishing in rural villages or temporary urban jobs rushed to retire. Between 1978 and 1983, the number of pensioners rose from three million to 12 million (see Table 2).

After 1984, several factors that had supported rapid growth declined in significance and impediments to further expansion appeared. The problems of unemployed youth became less pressing, managers were given greater autonomy to make profitability their guiding principle, and Chinese urbanites began to experience the first real surge of inflation since 1950. Nevertheless, with the exception of the decision to phase out the *dingti* option,[19] there were no efforts to reduce benefits or curtail eligibility; on the contrary, there was increased pressure to make retirement mandatory for women at 50 and men at 60[20] and benefit levels were repeatedly improved.[21] By the late 1980s, retirees equaled 25 percent of the labor force in the oldest industrial areas, and in some enterprises established before 1949, retirees outnumbered workers.[22] As a result, not only did the number of pensioners continue to grow exponentially, but by the end of the decade expenditures had almost quintupled (see Table 2).

TABLE 2
Growth in Number of Pensioners
and Outlays for Pensions

Year	Total Number of Pensioners (in millions)[a]	Cost (in billion *yuan*)	Ratio of Retirees to workers
1978	3.14 (2.84)	1.7	1:30.3
1979	5.96 (4.73)	3.2	1:16.7
1980	8.16 (6.38)	5.0	1:12.8
1981	9.50 (7.40)	6.2	1:11.5
1982	11.13 (8.65)	7.3	1:10.1
1983	12.92 (10.15)	8.7	1: 8.9
1984	14.78 (10.62)	10.6	1: 8.0
1985	16.37 (11.65)	14.9	1: 7.5
1986	18.05 (13.03)	19.4	1: 7.1
1987	19.68 (14.24)	23.8	1: 6.7
1988	21.15 (15.39)	32.0	1: 6.4
1989	22.01 (16.29)	38.2	1: 6.2
1990	23.01 (17.42)	47.2	1: 6.1

a: Number in parenthesis is the number of pensioners who were previously employees of state enterprises.

Source: *ZGTJNJ 1991*, 790 and 791.

As with the birth-control policy, the changes in pension programs followed different trajectories in rural and urban areas. For example, one survey of people over 60 found that less than 5 percent of all pension expenditures went to the almost 100 million rural residents of retirement age.[23] Thus, despite the massive growth in government expenditures for the elderly, rural elderly still depended overwhelmingly on their children or their own labor power. Moreover, to the extent that the Deng leaders publicly expressed any concern with the issue of rural pensions it was out of fear that financial inequalities between urban and rural elderly would encourage higher parity births among rural couples who needed sons for security in old age.[24] Yet in no instance that I have been able to find in the public record does a rural pension program offer coverage comparable to that of urban plans. Instead, new rural pensions follow a private life insurance model that requires high monthly contributions for only modest returns after 20 years of participation.[25]

In the cities, by contrast, pension reform after 1980 made lifetime pensions the norm. In the late 1970s, pensioners were a small male elite; by the early 1990s, women were as likely to receive pensions as men and the percentage of elderly with a pension equaled the percentage of the elderly population who had been workers or staff in urban enterprises.[26] In addition, not only did the 1980s witness an extraordinary increase in the availability and benefit level of urban pensions, but there were no efforts to reduce promises to the next generation of urban residents. The only reform in response to the growing financial burden was a 1989 decision to require modest contributions by individual employees into municipal-wide pension funds.[27] After a decade of efforts to expand the reach of the market and reduce the power of the command economy, the radical commitment of the communist revolution to guarantee the urban proletariat financial dependence in old age remained and was even extended to a wider group of urbanites.

By contrast, the Deng era brought little change to rural elderly. Pensions for peasants had been inconsequential in the late Mao era; they continued to be unimportant under Deng. Because urban benefits increased so rapidly, however, disparities between rural and urban strategies for preparing for old age widened. Urban parents do not raise children as the primary sources of financial support in old age, middle-aged urban women do not have to suffer abuse from husbands or sons in exchange for food and shelter in old age, and urban couples need not save and invest for life after retirement. As a result, not only do urban families differ from those in rural areas, but urban residents are more compromised in their support of the reform because they are more dependent on the old Maoist welfare state.

Changes in Educational Policies

During the Cultural Revolution decades, Maoist leaders were committed to leveling urban-rural educational differences. To achieve this goal they advocated a ten-year sequence of five-year primary schools combined with five-year general secondary schools. This reform eliminated the last year of primary school and erased the distinction between junior and senior high, a division that previously had distinguished superior from ordinary secondary education. Also, by first closing the universities and then re-opening them with an abbreviated curriculum, the Maoist policies eliminated clear payoffs for academic study in secondary school.

Under Deng, these Cultural Revolution policies were rapidly reversed. The old sequence of six years of primary school followed by three years of junior high and three years of senior high became the standard, and achievement-based entrance exams determined which students could advance to the next grade. Teacher's salaries were raised in an effort to increase their status and boost retention, and as a result a host of new extra fees were imposed for supplies and activities. After-school cram courses returned, and many parents felt it necessary to hire tutors in order that their children enter university or even an excellent secondary school.[28]

In terms of policy, the rejection of the abbreviated ten-year curriculum did not differentiate between rural and urban schools. Yet in practice, the outcomes were distinct. Many villages closed their secondary classes and kept only the reduced five-year primary curriculum in order to reduce local tax burdens. Village students who wanted to continue beyond primary school had to pass entrance exams for the more competitive secondary schools in market towns. Those who succeeded often benefited from the more rigorously academic junior and senior high school instruction; their parents also paid higher fees. The immediate result was, as one would expect, a decline in the percentage of students continuing to either junior or senior high (see Table 3).

TABLE 3
Promotion Rates

Year	To Jr. High	To Sr. High	To College*
1975	91%	60%	4%
1980	76%	46%	5%
1981	68%	32%	6%
1982	66%	32%	10%
1983	67%	36%	17%
1984	66%	38%	25%
1985	68%	42%	31%
1986	70%	41%	25%
1987	69%	39%	25%
1988	70%	38%	27%
1989	72%	38%	24%
1990	75%	41%	26%

* Percentage represents the number of June senior high graduates over the number of those entering the university in the following September.

Source: *ZGTJNJ 1991*, 701, 710, 716.

There also was a flurry of reports that high fees, as well as new opportunities to employ children in family farm tasks, discouraged rural parents from keeping children in school after they had acquired basic literacy and numeracy.[29] Since 1989, however, the picture has become a bit cloudier and it now seems that the damage to rural education may not have been as obvious as it seemed previously.[30]   There is a clear rural-urban gap, but the extent to which the difference increased after 1980 is difficult to measure. The more stratified, exam-oriented schools have benefited rural students by offering them better quality secondary schools.   In economically developed south China, where excellence in rural education has a long tradition, outstanding senior high schools have emerged in rural Guangdong, Fujian, Jiangsu, and Hubei.   When entrance exams for college were first reinstituted in the late 1970s, graduates of rural schools could rarely compete with the sent-down urban youth who had enjoyed excellent teaching in the early 1960s. By the late 1980s, the situation was more complicated.   Rural children as a whole were less likely to go beyond primary school than in 1985 (see Table 3), but those that did continue attended better schools, which prepared them more successfully to compete with urban peers in the college entrance exams.

It is also the case that unlike the pension programs that targeted virtually all state funds at the urban minority, rural education continued to preoccupy the central government both as a policy focus and as a financial responsibility.[31]   The central ministry did not release its authority to establish a standardized curriculum and state expenditures for education rose steadily, even eclipsing those for the military.[32]   Similarly, even as parents came to pay a higher percentage of educational charges, the central government increased the number of rural teachers on the state payroll and developed new competency exams to accredit rural teachers in an effort to raise standards.[33]

Conclusion

The Deng economic and political reforms launched after 1978 have dramatically changed Chinese society.   There is more commerce, more wealth, and more interaction with the world outside of China.   Incomes have doubled in real terms and a consumer revolution has made color television, motor-scooters, and karioke bars commonplace.   Nearly a half of rural China has new homes, and material expectations continue to rise.   Yet there have also been important continuities with the Maoist regime, and even with some Maoist ideals. Fertility has stabilized at the same level achieved during the late Mao era and generous, universal pensions remain a protected benefit for urban employees. The reach of the state is extensive, and dependency on subsidized public service creates conservative impulses even as the citizenry push for a more open polity and economy.

Yet coexistent with continuities are departures from the past that suggest further changes in the near future. A one-child family has become the norm throughout urban China, and large families of five and six children have all but disappeared in the countryside. Rural-urban boundaries have become increasingly blurred, and millions of rural residents formerly bound to small villages travel back and forth between rural and city life. Rural industry now produces half of the nation's industrial output, and private entrepreneurship, which had been reduced to a criminal activity under Mao, has emerged as a legitimate fast track for rural and urban youth.

The Deng social reforms have been modest, yet within the larger context of economic growth and change, even partial and compromised reforms tied to the Maoist past have shaped the opportunities of the future. The Maoist revolution repudiated the past; Deng and his reformers are more accommodating. Yet if the program of compromise and accommodation persists into a second decade of "reform," Chinese society may be more fundamentally changed than in previous decades of deliberate, radical trans-formation.

ENDNOTES

1. As of December 1978, 82 percent lived in villages where agriculture was the primary source of employment for the majority of adult males and females. *Zhongguo tongji nianjian 1991* (hereafter *ZGTJNJ 1991*) (Beijing: *Zhongguo tongji chubanshe*, 1991), 79.

2. As a result of the famine following the Great Leap Forward in 1958-60, natural rates of growth had been lower in 1960 and 1961, when CDR rose to 25.43 in 1960 and CBR plummeted to 18.02 in 1961. These low rates, however, were an aberration when placed in the context of long-term trends and, in contrast to the rates that prevailed in 1978, were short-term responses to horrific famines. *AGTJNJ 1991*, 79, 80.

3. In the early 1980s, CBR and CDR in France were 15 and 10, in Czechoslovakia 16 and 12, in the U.S.S.R. 19 and 10, and in the United States 16 and 9. By contrast, in India they were 36 and 15, in Indonesia 32 and 15, and Nigeria 50 and 17. *1983 World Population Data Sheet* (Washington, D.C.: Population Reference Bureau, 1983).

4. I realize that there are problems of consistent definition and accurate enumeration, and therefore deliberately compared *xiangcun* figures for these years because they seemed to capture the real limits on rural to urban migration. For discussion of the definitional issues, see Michael F. Martin, "Defining China's Rural Population," *China Quarterly* No. 130 (June 1992), 392-401. For statistics see *ZGTJNJ 1991*, 79.

5. H. Yuan Tien, "China's Demographic Dilemmas," *Population Bulletin* vol. 47, no. 1 (June 1992).

6. In 1978, when TFR had already fallen to 2.72, 42.5 percent of all births were third or a higher order. By 1985, only 19.7

80

percent were third or a higher order, and in 1990, 19.2 percent. Susan Greenhalgh, "Socialism and Fertility in China," *Annals, AAPSS*, no. 510 (July 1990), 79; *ZGTJNJ 1991*, 90.

7. Greenhalgh, "Socialism and Fertility in China," *Annals, AAPSS*, no. 510 (July 1990), 79; *ZGTJNJ 1991*, 90.

8. *Guowuyuan gongbao* 1989, 588-92; *Zhongguo laodong renshi bao*, 19 March 1986, 2; Dorothy Solinger, "Temporary Residence Certificates," *China Quarterly* no. 101 (March 1985), 98-100.

9. On impact of revised urban boundaries, see Goldstein, "Urbanization in China 1982-87"; on establishment of *zili kouliang hukou* for rural immigrants, see *Guofa* no. 141 (1984), *Guowuyuan gongbao* 1984, 919-20.

10. *RMRB*, 25 March 1990, 8.

11. In November 1980, a State Statistical Survey of 570,000 newborns found that 16.6 percent were born to unregistered immigrants, and the estimate nationwide was that there were at least 10 million migrant babies now resident in cities with their parents. *RMRB*, 23 May 1990, 6.

12. In a 12 December 1990 interview, Minister Peng Peiyun announced the total number of immigrants as 70 million, *RMRB*, 18 December 1990, 4.

13. *Mingbao*, 7 February 1990, 8.

14. *Mingbao* (Hong Kong), 27 June 1989, 9; 7 January 1990, 25; 19 January 1991, 7; *RMRB*, 14 August 1988, 8; 4 March 1989, 2.

15. *Employment and Economic Growth in Urban China 1949-57* (Cambridge: Cambridge University Press, 1971), 65.

16. Between 1951-60, net migration flows were 30/1,000 to cities; between 1961 and 1965, it was 18/1,000 out of the cities. Lavely, Lee, and Wang, *Journal of Asian Studies* November

1990, 814. From Shanghai alone 800,000 urbanites were sent down in 1955, and in 1957-58 another one million were permanently relocated out of the city. Howe, *Employment and Economic Growth*, 132.

17. Deborah Davis-Friedmann, *Long Lives: Chinese Elderly and the Communist Revolution*, expanded edition (Stanford, Calif.: Stanford University Press, 1991), 15-33, 85-101; Deborah Davis, "Chinese Social Welfare," *China Quarterly* no. 119 (September 1989), 577-97; Gail Henderson, "Public Health in China," *China Briefing 1992*, 103-123.

18. Davis-Friedmann, *Long Lives* (expanded edition), 107-116.

19. *Guofa* #137 in 1983 officially repealed routine use of *dingti*. Between 1984 and 1985 it was phased out in most state enterprises, although units still carried a responsibility for employee dependents who could find no job, and in some cases the term *dingti* persisted when a child joined an enterprise after the parent retired. *Guowuyuan gongbao*, 29 November 1983, 931-33; *Zhongguo jiaoyu bao*, 5 February 1985, 1; *Jingji yu guanli yanjiu*, no. 2 (1986), 28-30; *Beijing Review*, 21 August 1989, 4-5; *RMRB*, 5 May 1992, 5.

20. Women who held white collar jobs only reached mandatory retirement age at 55 if they could claim cadre status, and by the end of the decade, women professionals, like their male counterparts, were only required to retire at 60. For the vast majority of women who were manual or routine clerical workers, however, 50 remained the mandatory age of retirement. Similarly, efforts were made to prevent higher rank male cadre and professionals from working beyond mandatory ages. *Zhongguo funu* no. 9 (1990), 39; Xu Jin, "Discussion of retirement system and retirement ages," *Renkou yu jingji* no. 2 (1992), 54-57; *RMRB*, 18 June 1992, 3.

21. For example, in 1989 *Guofa* no. 83 raised all pensions by one step (or at least eight *yuan*) and in 1992 base pensions were

increased for those who failed to participate in the 1985 wage increases, and all retirees then received an across-the-board increase of 10 percent or a minimum increase of 120 *yuan* per year. *Zhonghua laonianbao*, 13 June 1990, 1; *Xinmin wanbao* (Shanghai), 24 July 1992, 1.

22. *Zhongguo laodong renshi bao*, 7 June 1986, 1; *Xinhua ribao*, 10 December 1985, 1; *Zhongguo Laodong* no. 8 (1985), 24; Li Dafu, "In regard to unified management of pension funds," *Fujian lilun* no. 12 (1985, 58-60; *Caizheng* no. 8 (1985), 28-29; *RMRB*, 9 June 1985, 2.

23. Bai Baoshan and Zhao Zhijie, "Discussion of Population Aging and the Development of a New Old Age Insurance System," *Kexue zhanxian* no. 4 (1991), 126-31.

24. The primary targets have been young employees of the new township industries and parents of single daughters in wealthy villages. The one exception to this have been efforts for village cadres, which, however, have been the source of resentment by both overtaxed villagers and older cadres with no pensions. *RMRB*, 3 July 1990, 2; 8 May 1991, 3; 15 June 1991, 5; 14 June 1992, 1.

25. *Beijing Review*, 12 March 1990, 24; *RMRB* 3 July 1990, 2; and 15 June 1991, 5.

26. Davis-Friedmann, *Long Lives* (expanded edition), 113.

27. Typically, individual contributions were set at 1-3 percent of basic monthly wage. *Guofa* no. 24 (1989), *Guowuyuan gongbao*, 13 May 1989, 233-42; *Mingbao*, 9 April 1991, 7; *Guofa* no. 33 (1991), *Guowuyuan*, 11 September 1991, 967-70.

28. In 1992, it was estimated that 30 percent of Shanghai students who sat for year-end exams in primary and secondary schools hired private tutors. *Mingbao*, 14 August 1992, 73.

29. Zhang Guangxi, "Divide the Schools and Split the Management," *Renmin jiaoyu* no. 8 (1985), 4–5; *RMRB*, 23 November 1986, 3; 17 June 1987, 5; 25 November 1987, 3; 31 May 1988, 3; 3 June 1988, 3; 10 July 1988, 2.

30. Davis, "Chinese Social Welfare," *The China Quarterly*, 581–85.

31. See, for example, the annual report of the State Education Council, in *RMRB*, 24 June 1990, 3, and the passage of new education surtax to go into effect August 1990, *RMRB*, 14 June 1990, 3.

32. According to the SEC report cited above, public funds as a percentage of total expenditures for secondary education fell from 35.3 percent in 1985 to 23.5 percent in 1988; for primary education the reduction was from 24.3 percent to 14.9 percent. *RMRB*, 24 June 1990, 3. Between 1985 and 1988, however, total expenditures for culture and education rose from 89.5 billion *yuan* to 13.97 billion, while those for the military rose only from 19.1 billion to 21.8 billion. By contrast, ten years earlier in 1978 the military had outspent education 16.7 billion to 7 billion. *ZGTJNJ 1991*, 214.

33. *Zhongguo jiaoyubao*, 18 November, 1989, 1; 7 December 1989, 2.

CHAPTER FOUR

Legal Reform in Deng's China

SHAO-CHUAN LENG

Since the initiation of reforms by Deng Xiaoping in 1978, socialist legality and *Fazhi* have been used more frequently than any other terms of reference in the PRC, except for the four modernizations. This chapter will begin with an examination of motivations and measures of Deng's legal reform. Then it will proceed to discuss the limits and problems of the reform. Finally, it will assess current trends and future prospects regarding the rule of law in China.

Reasons for and Measures of Legal Reform

As in the case of *Fa* (positive law) and *Li* (moral code or customary law) in traditional China, there has been a competitive coexistence of jural (formal) and societal (informal) models of law in the People's Republic of China to regulate human behavior and social order. The jural model stands for formal, elaborate, and codified rules enforced by a centralized and institutionalized bureaucracy, while the societal model focuses on socially approved norms and values inculcated by political socialization and enforced by extrajudicial apparatuses consisting of administrative agencies and social organizations.

The entire legal experience of China under Mao Zedong bore his strong personal imprint with a clear emphasis on class justice, mass line tactics, the party's dominant role, rule by man over rule

85

by law, and the societal model of law over the jural model. There was a short period, 1954-1957, when the PRC was moving in the direction of legal stability and codification following the Soviet model. This move, however, came to an abrupt end in 1957 with the launching of the Anti-Rightist Campaign. The formal legal structure suffered even more serious damage from the Cultural Revolution when most offenses and disputes were handled by extrajudicial institutions, resulting in abuses, excesses, and a "state of lawlessness."[1]

Since the emergence of Deng Xiaoping's leadership in 1978, the PRC has taken steps to institute law reform and to develop a "socialist legality with Chinese characteristics." The tone was set by the Communique of the Third Plenum of the 11th Central Committee of the Chinese Communist Party (22 December 1978):

> In order to safeguard people's democracy, it is imperative to strengthen the socialist legal system so that democracy is systematized and written in such a way as to insure the stability, continuity and full authority of this democratic system and these laws; *there must be laws for people to follow, these laws must be observed, their enforcement must be strict and law breakers must be dealt with.*[2]

Obviously, this policy of legal reform has been closely linked to the commitment of Deng's China to the program of four modernizations. The PRC needs a formal legal system to ensure a secure and orderly environment, essential to the successful development of its economy. It also expects a growing demand for economic legislation to regulate production processes and the relationships among production units. Moreover, China must project itself as a stable and orderly society with effective laws to protect the interests and rights of foreigners in order to expand trade, import advanced technology, and attract international investment. Deng said in early 1986: "We must use two hands to carry on the four modernizations: grasping construction with one hand and grasping the legal system with the other."[3]

Since 1978 the PRC has undertaken a series of measures to develop the legal system. First of all, a new and relatively liberal constitution was enacted in 1982. As the PRC's fourth state constitution, it contains provisions instituting socialist legality and guaranteeing individual rights and freedoms, including equality before the law. Article 5 of the constitution requires all organs of state, all political parties, and all organizations and institutions to abide by the constitution and the law. Articles 126 and 131 stipulate that people's courts and people's procuratorates exercise their respective authority independently according to law and are not subject to interference by administrative organs, public organizations, or individuals. One key constraint, however, contained in the constitution (Preamble) is that the legal system, like China's other institutions, is expected to operate within the confines of the four cardinal principles, namely, the socialist road, the people's dictatorship, the leadership of the CCP, and Marxism-Leninism-Mao Zedong Thought.[4]

Other steps that have been taken to build socialist legality include the reorganization and expansion of the formal legal institutions. The restructured four-level court system, for instance, is composed of the Supreme People's Court, the 31 higher people's courts, the 377 intermediate people's courts (including military and other special courts), and the 3,015 basic people's courts (including special courts).[5] The current organic law contains provisions concerning judicial independence, equality before the law, public (open) trials, the right to defense, people's assessors, the collegiate system, adjudication (judicial) committees, and the two-trial (one appeal) system. The new law makes the court accountable only to the people's congress and frees the court from direct supervision by local government (Articles 35-36).

With a hierarchy parallel to that of the courts, the procuracy was reinstituted in 1978. Among the functions of the procuracy are investigation, prosecution, scrutinizing trial procedures, and overseeing the execution of judgments and operations of prisons. Resurrection of the Chinese bar has also been an important aspect of law reform in Deng's China. According to the 1980 Provisional Act on Lawyers, China's lawyers are the "state's legal workers" and have the duty to "safeguard the interests of the State, the collectives and the legitimate rights and interests of citizens" (Article 1). Legal advisers' offices (law firms) are the work organs of people's lawyers.

Each office oversees the professional activities of lawyers, collects fees from its clients, and distributes work to its members.

Another significant aspect of China's legal reform under Deng has been the restoration and expansion of legal education. There are in the PRC departments of law at 51 universities and 27 colleges, one political-legal university (China Political-Legal University), and four political-legal institutes. In addition, the Ministry of Justice has established 28 judicial schools, 27 political-legal cadre schools, and other ad-hoc short-term institutes for judicial personnel. As a part of the nationwide movement to propagate legal knowledge, new courses of law are now offered in all Chinese universities and schools.[6] Legal research and publications have also flourished under Deng's reform. Numerous books, monographs, journals, and even a legal system daily have appeared on the scene.

It is in the area of its legislative output that the PRC has proceeded with surprising speed. In the last 14 years the National People's Congress and its standing committee have adopted 130 laws and regulations and 80 resolutions and decisions on legal matters. During the same period the State Council has issued some 900 administrative regulations and decrees while the authorities at the provincial level have adopted over 1,000 local laws and regulations. Among the major enactments were Organic Laws, Criminal Law, Criminal Procedure Law, Civil Procedure Law, Civil Law General Principles, and Administrative Procedure Law.[7]

In an effort to invigorate the domestic economy and to implement the open-door policy, the PRC has specifically quickened the pace of economic legislation. The NPC and its standing committee and the State Council have promulgated over 300 economic laws and regulations in recent years. The majority of them deal with China's foreign economic relations and trade.

What has emerged from the legal reform in Deng's China is "socialist legality" with Chinese characteristics. As stated by Chinese leaders and legal experts, their socialist laws must be based on the contemporary and historical realities of China. So by proceeding from the actual conditions of China and acting according to the principles of socialist legality, the PRC is said to be establishing a "Chinese-style socialist legal system."[8]

Fully in line with the Chinese Li-Fa tradition, Beijing has also given due attention to both jural and societal models of law. Parallel to the restructured judicial system, there are in China public security organs and other extrajudicial apparatus that continue to play important roles in maintaining law and order, imposing sanctions, and settling disputes. The frequent use of "circumstances," without any specific listing, in determining penalties in China's Criminal Law, and the practice of combining punishment with education in its penal policy including the suspension of the death sentence for two years are just a few examples marked with pronounced Chinese characteristics.[9]   In civil matters, dispute resolution through mediation is known to have a long history in China. This traditional preference for informal means to handle civil matters is also manifested both in law and practice in the current Chinese approach to domestic civil disputes and to disputes involving foreign economic and trade activities.[10]

On the whole, Deng's China has made considerable progress in its efforts to restore the respectability of the jural model of law and to provide some measure of stability and predictability of its renovated legal system. Conceptually, however, Chinese socialist legality still shares certain common features with the bureaucratic-style Soviet legal system, namely, law as an instrument imposed by the state on society, serving the interests of socialism and Party Rule.[11] The term *fazhi* really means "rule by law" rather than "rule of law," and the phrase *yi fa zhi guo* suggests "using the law to rule the country" and not "running state affairs according to the law." Both in theory and in practice, the current Chinese legal system leaves much to be desired if measured by the general standards of the rule of law.

There have been at times some encouraging signs of the PRC's attempt to move beyond the bureaucratic mould (Soviet or Chinese legalist version) in developing "socialist legality with Chinese characteristics."   In his speech on "emancipate the mind . . ." in 1978, Deng Xiaoping rejected in no uncertain terms the practice of *renzhi* (rule of man):

Democracy has to be institutionalized and written into law, so as to make sure that institutions and laws do not

89

change whenever the leadership changes or whenever the leaders change their views. . . . Very often what leaders say is taken as law and anyone who disagrees is called a lawbreaker. Such law changes whenever a leader's views change.[12]

Legal publications and professional conferences in the 1980s (before the Tiananmen tragedy of June 1989) showed an interesting trend of "emancipation of mind," as academics and experts discussed and debated openly certain touchy issues, apparently with the toleration, if not the blessing, of the Communist regime. Some rejected the traditional Marxist view on the class nature of law by maintaining that law cannot be considered a product of class struggle nor as peculiar to class society.[13] Others took on the question of *yi fa zhi guo.* The majority argued for the rule of law as against the rule by law. According to them, the latter represented the ancient legalist prescription whereby law was used as a bureaucratic instrument by feudal lords and kings to rule the masses; in contrast, under the genuine rule of law, the people should be regarded as the essence and law must be viewed as a rule of conduct binding on all, including political leaders.[14]

Limits and Problems of the Reform

In spite of some apparent progress in China's legal reform efforts, there are limits to the reform and a number of basic problems and difficulties in the PRC's move toward the rule of law. First of all, there is an acute shortage of trained personnel in the legal field despite some improvement in coping with this glaring weakness. With a population of over one billion, China has only 380,014 judicial personnel (200,134 in courts and 179,870 in procuratorates) and 50,000 lawyers.[15]

Second, both the populace and bureaucracy tend to have an indifferent and skeptical attitude toward law, as "legal illiteracy" and old beliefs cannot be overcome overnight. Harassment of lawyers is a case in point. Many people consider lawyers as "those who speak for criminals." Some officials regard arguments from lawyers as challenges to their authority. Not only has lawyers' work been obstructed by state and party cadres, but they have also been expelled from the courtroom, arrested, and persecuted, as reported by the press.[16]

The problem confronting China, as noted by the late Jurist Zhang Youyu, "is not the lack of laws but failure to implement them.[17] Official abuses of power have continued in the form of illegal arrests, unlawful detentions, and interference with judicial work.[18] Moreover, the NPC Standing Committee revived in 1980 the police's power to apply a wide range of "administrative" sanctions, by which the police can send offenders to reeducation through labor camps without trial for a period of one to four years.[19] Also through a measure known as "sheltering for examination" (*shourong shencha*), the police can detain people for investigation for an extended time without a formal charge.[20]

Finally, the fundamental problem confronting the PRC's law reform remains the relationship between the Party and the legal system. Technically, the Party and its members must all work within the confines of the constitution and the law. In practice, Party officials too often let political considerations prevail over legal requirements. Take, for example, the principle of judicial independence guaranteed by the constitution and the law. Although the practice of Party Committee secretaries reviewing and approving cases in Mao's China has been discontinued, the people's court still has to seek guidance from the Party Committee on broad policy matters and on important or complex cases. In addition, the procedure of adjudication supervision, which allows liberal reopening of official judgments, further places enormous institutional constraints on individual judicial work.[21]

In recent years the PRC has been beset by a rising number of economic offenses, with many offenders being party and government officials and their relatives. Beijing's fight against economic crimes has been complicated by the persistent practice of favoring people of power, influence, and connections without regard to the principle of equality before the law. Official corruption and irregularities were one of the major complaints of student protesters in the 1989 Tiananmen pro-democracy movement.

Lately, the fight against corruption and bribery is the top priority of China's law enforcement agencies. As reported by Deputy Procurator-General Liang Guoqing, in the first four months of 1993 the procuratorial organs had handled 13,729 corruption and bribery cases, of which 6,097 had been investigated, 4,570 solved, and 5,384 people brought to trial, with 158 million yuan of embezzled money recovered.[22] According to Ren Jianxin, president of the Supreme People's Court, whoever commits a crime will be prosecuted, tried, and punished to the full extent regardless of his high position.[23] Yet there is no report of efforts to check certain "dubious" economic activities of the "princes clique." Some cases that may show the regime or its leaders in a poor light have been dealt with leniently or given a news blackout.[24]

All in all, the overriding restriction on China's legal development continues to be the dictates of politics. Like other institutions in the PRC, the legal system is expected to operate within the so-called Four Cardinal Principles, namely, the socialist road, the People's Democratic Dictatorship, the leadership of the CCP, and Marxism-Leninism-Mao Zedong thought. Whenever these principles are perceived by the Chinese elites as being threatened, legal niceties are set aside. The treatment of political dissidents and student demonstrations is a case in point.

After some initial toleration of free expression in 1978-79, the Chinese government then proceeded to close the Democracy Wall and arrested, tried, and imprisoned a number of dissidents, notably Wei Jingsheng, who called for the "fifth modernization"—democracy. Subsequently, the campaigns against "spiritual pollution" in 1983-84 and "bourgeois liberalization" in 1986-87 were all undertaken in the name of upholding the Four Cardinal Principles. Still, the violent crackdown on the pro-democracy movement on 4 June 1989 came as a great shock, which appears to have undone much of what Deng Xiaoping and his reform-minded associates had accomplished since 1978.[25]

Immediately following the military crackdown, there were reports of arbitrary arrest and detention of thousands of protesters, who were subject to all types of abuses, including torture and administrative sanctions. All told, little regard was given to the procedural protections provided by the constitution and the

Criminal Procedure Law in Beijing's dealing with the participants of the pro-democracy movement.[26] The Communist authorities decided in early 1990 to lift martial law and later began to release periodically a number of detained activists. In the midst of tight political control and uncertainty, the Administrative Procedure Law, which permits individuals to challenge and sue administrative agencies, came into force in China in October 1990 with much fanfare.[27]

Trials of pro-democracy activists took place in early 1991. Altogether, 18 dissidents were sentenced to prison terms ranging from two to 13 years, while 69 others were released. Beijing described all these trials and sentences as fair by "combining punishment with leniency," but by international standards the activists committed no criminal offense and were only exercising their basic rights of free speech, assembly, and demonstration guaranteed by Article 35 of the PRC's own constitution. The trials were conducted more like a sentence-announcing meeting. No independent observers were present, nor was there any meaningful defense for the accused. The pressure on the defendants to confess and repent was enormous under the PRC's policy of "leniency to those who confess and severity to those who resist."[28]

In response to international criticism and pressure, the PRC published a "White Paper on Human Rights in China" in 1991.[29] The paper defended China's judicial work and stressed the accomplishments of its human rights record, especially in economic and social development. However unpersuasive Chinese arguments may have appeared to international critics, publication of this paper certainly reflected PRC leaders' defensive mentality trying hard to rationalize their policies. Moreover, this also showed the reluctant admission and awareness by the Chinese leadership of the existence of a universal norm and consensus on human rights acceptable to countries of diverse backgrounds and conditions.[30]

Current Trends and Future Prospects

Tiananmen notwithstanding, the Communist regime has continued to emphasize its commitment to economic reform and open-door policies, which received a special boost by Deng Xiaoping's well-publicized visit to the south in early 1992.[31] Coordinated with the current momentum of economic development is the PRC's renewed stress on legal reform. After all, in order to achieve the goal of modernization, Deng's China must restore some measure of credibility both at home and abroad by showing its genuine attempt to establish socialist legality.

Wan Li, chairman of the NPC Standing Committee, stated in 1992: "The policy of reform and opening up urgently needs the impetus and guarantee of democracy and the legal system. . . . All judicial personnel are required to firmly establish the concept that all men are equal before the law, and no one is allowed to obtain any privilege or freedom beyond the limits of the constitution and law."[32] In his report to the National People's Congress in March 1993, Li Peng had this to say: We should strengthen the legal system, especially legislation dealing with economic matters, so as to institutionalize successful experiments in reform and codify sound policies, to consolidate our achievements and to ensure that the reform proceeds well."[33]

According to the State Council's plan for 1993 legislative work, 89 pieces of law (17 laws and 72 administrative statutes) will be submitted for consideration this year. They cover mainly the following fields: (1) standardizing and maintaining market economic order; (2) strengthening social security and safeguarding people's legitimate rights and interests; (3) tightening macro-economic regulation and control; (4) ensuring the process of opening to the outside world; and (5) improving administrative organizations and promoting clean administration.[34]

In line with the intensive move toward economic reform, the National People's Congress made several constitutional amendments in March 1993. A most significant amendment was to replace in Article 15 the clause "the country will practice a planned economy" with "the state practices a socialist market economy." The term *state-run enterprises* was also replaced by *state-owned enterprises* in Articles 16 and 17. Moreover, the wording of "rural people's communes and agricultural producers' cooperatives" in Article 8 was changed to "the responsibility system, the main form of which is household contracts linking remuneration to output." Politically, as expected, Deng Xiaoping's "four cardinal principles" were retained in the Preamble of the Constitution. Not ready for the Western multiparty system, the Chinese substitute was the following addition to the Preamble: "The system of multiparty cooperation and political consultation led by the Communist Party of China will exist and develop in China for a long time to come."[35]

While much remains to be done for the PRC's human rights situation to meet international standards, Chinese society appears to be more open and relaxed today than before. There have been indications that China plans to replace its controversial counter-revolutionary offense with the "crime of endangering state security" to be in line with internationally accepted legal practice and convention.[36] The PRC is also reported to be in the process of drafting its first press law.[37] Furthermore, the Ministry of Justice has a plan to reform the system of lawyers in China. According to Minister Xiao Yang, the plan is to triple the number of lawyers from the present 50,000 to 150,000 by the turn of the century. In his words, China needs at least 300,000 lawyers who are legal workers not only for the state but also for the society responsible for protecting clients' legal interests and advising on the country's laws. The reform plan will make Chinese lawyers no longer restricted by ownerships approved by the state. They will be given more freedom in their practice of law, be allowed to join in legal partnerships, and be able to advise clients on their own account. They will not be paid by the state and will be allowed to charge clients fees for legal advice. In addition, Chinese lawyers are to be allowed to establish offices overseas and foreign firms will be allowed to set up in China.[38]

Another encouraging development is the latest trend to have liberal views on sensitive issues published in China's leading legal journals and newspapers. Some publications, for example, openly endorse principles essential to the Western legal system, namely, supremacy of the law, protection of individual liberties and rights, limited government, and separation of powers.[39] Others urge the emancipation of mind and bold absorption of the best from the Western legal experience and institutions, including the concept of human rights, in support of the reform and open-door policies.[40] Dagong Bao (L'Impartial Daily) recently ran two articles originally published in China's *Social Science Journal* that criticize the "outmoded" idea of a supreme leader over the law and call for the rule of law to guarantee the principle of due process and to ensure tolerance and respect for the minority.[41]

Probably, the most hopeful sign is the PRC's changing economic landscape brought about by Deng's reform policy. Intended or not, it is in the process of creating socioeconomic pluralism in China—a precondition necessary to the rule of law as suggested by Professor Robert Unger in the book *Law in Modern Society.*[42]

As a result of economic reform, there has been an important change in the structure of the Chinese economy. The state-owned sector now accounts for only 51 percent of China's total industrial production value, down from 76 percent in 1980. The nonstate sectors have increased their shares substantially: about 37 percent for the collective sector and 12 percent for the private sector and foreign-funded firms. The projected shares in the year 2000 are 27.2 percent for the state sector, 47.7 percent for the collective sector, and 25.1 percent for the private sector and foreign-funded enterprises.[43] Of the total industrial output value in 1992, the state sector was up 12.6 percent, collective enterprises up 28.5 percent, and private and foreign-funded enterprises up 48.8 percent.[44]

While economic reform has led to greater roles for the private and other nonstate sectors in the Chinese economy, the "open door" policy has expanded economic, commercial, cultural, and legal contacts and dealings between the PRC and foreign countries. There are 190 countries and regions with which China has forged trade and economic ties. The total value of Chinese foreign trade in 1992 reached $165.6 billion, doubling that in 1988 and placing China as the 11th largest trading country in the world. The PRC has adopted more than 200 laws and regulations governing its foreign economic and trade relations.[45] Prominent among them are those concerning joint ventures, taxation, foreign economic contracts, technology imports, trademarks, patent rights, etc.

Deng Xiaoping's dramatic visit to South China in early 1992 to publicize a new round of reform has not only triggered the rapid growth of the Chinese economy but has also reportedly inspired important changes in values and behavior patterns in the entire society.[46]   Borrowing from the West has been encouraged by the official media. According to an article in the *People's Daily*, China need not fear Western cultural subversion but should promote more exchanges to "enrich our culture." Aside from foreign capital, technology, and management expertise, it says, China should consider copying "capitalistic economic policies and legislation that reflect laws of reality."[47]   An article on the "New Meaning of 'Take-ism'" in *Party School Tribune Monthly* suggests that the absorption and assimilation of the fruits of human civilization, including all advanced operative and management methods developed in capitalist nations, is "an important component of our party's theory of opening up to the outside." China's development, as is pointed out, cannot be divorced from the world; we must "allow ourselves up to 'take' from others so that we can accelerate the pace of our modernization."[48]   More important, Deng's reform and open-door policies have been officially endorsed by the 14th Party Congress and by the 8th National People's Congress. A group of relatively young, well-educated, and reform-minded leaders are now also in place to continue Deng's programs.

On the other hand, desire for retaining power and concern with political instability remain major factors accounting for the unwillingness of Chinese leaders to reform the political system, which in turn continues to inhibit a clear and total commitment to thorough-going legal reform in China. There is, however, reason for optimism about the future. Given the momentum of Deng's policies, continued economic and social changes in the country will most likely pave the way for a gradual but inevitable political change and also accelerate the pace of China's long march to the rule of law.

ENDNOTES

1. See Shao-chuan Leng and Hungdah Chiu, *Criminal Justice in Post-Mao China* (Albany: State University of New York Press, 1985), chap. 2; also Shao-chuan Leng, "The Role of Law in the People's Republic of China as Reflecting Mao's Influence," *Journal of Criminal Law and Criminology* 68, no. 3 (1977): 356-73.

2. *The China Quarterly*, no. 77 (March 1979): 172.

3. The statement is quoted in Commentator, "The Legal System and Construction," *Liaowang* (Outlook) (17 February 1986): 4.

4. Text of the constitution is in *Renmin Ribao* (People's Daily), 5 December 1982, 1-4; its English translation is in FBIS (Foreign Broadcast Information Service), *Daily Report: China*, 7 December 1982, K1-K28.

5. *Zhongguo Falu Nianjian 1992* (Chinese Law Yearbook 1992) (Beijing: Legal Press, 1992), 858.

6. *People's Republic of China Year Book, 1988/89* (Beijing: China Year Book LTD., 1988), 178; ibid., *1990/91*, 113.

7. *Fazhi Ribao* (Legal System Daily), 10 March 1993, 1; *Beijing Review* (33) 30 July-5 August 1990, 21.

8. "Gist of Peng Zhen's Speech on Civil Code," FBIS, *Daily Report: China* (29 May 1986): K12-K13; Xiang Chunyi et al., "Making Effort to Establish a Chinese-Style Socialist Legal System," *Honggi* (Red Flag), no. 3 (1984): 2-12, 18.

9. Leng and Chiu, 127-28, 142-43.

10. According to Zhang Youyu, for example, "up to 90 percent of the civil cases have been resolved through mediation in the past few years," XINHUA, 8 March 1983.

11. See Leng and Chiu, 52-53; Bernard A. Ramundo, *The Soviet Legal System: A Primer* (Chicago: American Bar Association, 1971), 6-7.

12. Deng Xiaoping, "Emancipate the mind, seek the truth from fact and unite as one in looking to the future," Selected Works of *Deng Xiaoping (1975-1982)* (Beijing: Foreign Languages Press, 1984), 157-58.

13. Zhang Zonghou, "Query about the Three Basic Concepts of Law," *Faxue* (Law Science), no. 1 (1986): 2-7; Zhou Fengju, "Is Law Simply An Instrument of Class Struggle?" *Faxue Yanjiu* (Studies in Law), no. 1 (1980): 40.

14. Ni Zhengmao, "On the Requirements of the Legal System in Political Restructuring," *Faxue Jikan* (Law Science Quarterly), no. 2 (1987): 3. At a Party conference in January 1985, the concept "rule-by-law state" was reportedly abandoned in favor of "depending-on-the-law state." See Ronald C. Keith, "Chinese Politics and the New Theory of 'Rule of Law'," *The China Quarterly* (June 1991): 115-116.

15. *Zhongguo Falu Nianjian 1992*, 859, 861; *China Daily*, 22 July 1993, 3.

16. Victor Fund, "China's Lawyers Suffer from Low Status," *Asian Wall Street Journal*, 13 April 1987, 1; "How Can You Say the 'Lawyers Only Speak for Criminal Element'?" *Renmin Ribao*, 25 September 1986, 4.

17. *Beijing Ribao*, 14 February 1986, 1.

18. See, for instance, Department of State Report, *Country Reports*

on *Human Rights Practice for 1991* (Washington, D.C.: U.S. Government Printing Office, 1992), 812.

19. *Renmin Ribao*, 24 February 1980, 4.

20. For this extrajudicial means of detention, see Tao-tai Hsia and Wendy Zeldin, "Sheltering for Examination in the Legal System of the People's Republic of China," *China Law Reporter* II, no. 2 (1992): 95-128.

21. See Margaret Y. K. Woo, "Adjudication Supervision and Judicial Independence in the P.R.C.," *American Journal of Comparative Law* 39 (Winter 1991): 115-116.

22. *Beijing Review* 36 (28 June-4 July 1993): 6.

23. *Chung-yang Jih-pao* (Central Daily News), Overseas edition, 1 August 1993, 4.

24. For instance, a news blackout has been imposed on the trial of Yu Zuomin, the head of Daqiuzhuang rural-enterprise conglomerate. Yu is reportedly a crony of the Deng family. Ibid.; *South China Morning Post*, 30 June 1993, 1.

25. For the Tiananmen tragedy, consult Andrew Nathan, *China's Crisis* (New York: Columbia University Press, 1990), 171-92; Lee Feigon, *China Rising: The Meaning of Tiananmen* (Chicago: I. R. Dee, 1990).

26. See Department of State Report, *Country Reports on Human Rights Practices for 1989* (Washington, D.C.: U.S. Government Printing Office, 1990), 803-907; James Feinerman, "Deteriorating Human Rights in China," *Current History*, September 1990; Asia Watch, *Punishment Season: Human Rights in China after Martial Law* (New York: Asia Watch, 1990).

27. An analysis of the Administrative Procedure Law is in Jyh-pin Fa and Shao-chuan Leng, "Judicial Review of Administration

in the People's Republic of China," *Case Western Reserve Journal of International Law* 23, no. 3 (Summer 1991): 447-62.

28. For a detailed analysis of these trials, see Tao-tai Hsia and Wendy Zeldin, "Justice and Human Rights in China: Criminal Trials of the Leading 1989 Pro-Democracy Activists." Far Eastern Law Division, Library of Congress, February 1991, 51 (mimeographed).

29. English text is in FBIS, *China: Daily Report Supplement* (21 November 1991): 1-29.

30. For a discussion of the issue of human rights, consult the Stanley Foundation, "Human Rights and U.S. Policy," *The Eighteenth Strategy for Peace Conference Report*, 13-16 October 1977, 14-16; Isaiah Berlin, "Two Concepts of Liberty," *Four Essays on Liberty* (London: Oxford University Press, 1969), 118-72; Randle Edwards, Louis Henkin, Andrew Nathan, *Human Rights in Contemporary China* (New York: Columbia University Press, 1986), 1-2, 7-13.

31. "China Swings Back to Reform," *The Economist*, 1 February 1992, 35-36.

32. Chen Shao-pin, "Wan Li Talks about 'Democracy and Legal System'," *Ching Pao*, Hong Kong, 5 January 1992, 46; FBIS, *Daily Report: China*, 21 January 1992, 34.

33. "Report on the Work of the Government," *Beijing Review* 36 (12-18 April 1993): XIII.

34. "Reporters Briefed on Council's Legislative Work," FBIS, *Daily Report: China*, 19 May 1993, 23.

35. "Amendments to Constitution Published," FBIS, *Daily Report: China*, 30 March 1993, 42-43; *Beijing Review* 36 (26 April-2 May 1993): 14-16; *South China Morning Post*, 25 March 1993, 10.

36. *South China Morning Post*, 22 May 1993, 8; FBIS, *Daily Report*, 18 May 1993, 19.

37. Ibid.

38. *Liaowang*, 12 July 1993, 6-7; FBIS, *Daily Report: China*, 28 June 1993, 32.

39. Yang Haikun, "Theory and Practice of Chinese Socialist Legal System," *Faxue Yanjiu*, no. 1 (1993): 9-14, 42; Zhao Changsheng, "Reform and Modernization of the Chinese Legal System," *Falu Kexue* (Science of Law), no. 4 (1992): 3-8.

40. Chen Guangzhong, "Strengthening Human Rights Protection is needed in Reform and Open Door Policies," *ZhongGuo Faxue* (Chinese Legal Science), no. 4 (1992): 18-19; Chen Chuenlong, "Take One Step forward to Emancipate Mind and Expand legal Studies," *Faxue Yanjiu*, no. 5 (1992): 1-2.

41. *Dagong Bao*, Hong Kong, 1 December 1992, 8; 8 December 1992, 20. English translation of the articles is in *Inside China Mainland*, Taipei, February 1993, 20-24.

42. For Unger's discussion of the prerequisites for a pluralistic legal order to develop, see *Law in Modern Society* (New York: Macmillan, 1976), 52-53, 66-76; for an interesting analysis of the march of pluralism in the PRC according to Unger's definition, see Richard Baum, "Modernization and Legal Reform Post-Mao China: The Rebirth of Socialist Legality," *Studies in Comparative Communism* 19, no. 2 (Summer 1986): 94-103.

43. "Private Sector Now Key Factor in Economy," *China Daily*, 6 August 1993, 1; "Table III on Chinese Economy Based on the Estimates of the Chinese Information Center," *Chung-kung Yen-chiu* (Studies on Chinese Communism) (15 November 1992): 79.

44. *Beijing Review* 36 (8-14 March 1993): 33.

45. *Beijing Review* 36 (22-28 February 1993): 5; "China Is Taking Giant Steps to Become a Major Trading Power in the World," *Liaowang*, 10 May 1993, 7-8.

46. A report released by the Sociology Study Institute of the Chinese Academy of Social Sciences outlines six prominent social changes that have taken place in China as a result. See "Significant Social Changes Since 1992," *Beijing Review* 36 (21-27 June 1993): 34.

47. Fang Sheng, "Opening to the Outside World and Making Use of Capitalism," *Renmin Ribao*, 23 February 1992, 1.

48. *Party School Tribune Monthly* (5 October 1992): 59-62; *Inside China Mainland*, March 1993, 21-25.

CHAPTER FIVE

A Tentative Appraisal of China's Military Reforms*

PAUL H. B. GODWIN

Introduction

Even a tentative appraisal of the military reforms by Deng Xiaoping since the late 1970s suffers from severe problems of measurement. No one not intimately familiar with the Chinese armed forces prior to Deng's reform efforts is really sure of the condition of the Chinese defense establishment before the reforms were undertaken. All we do know is that Deng himself was profoundly disturbed by the condition of the armed forces in the mid-1970s and that their military operations in the brief 1979 war with Vietnam were far less than satisfactory. Nonetheless, the mere fact that Deng found it necessary to undertake a complete overhaul of the entire Chinese defense establishment—from recruitment and training of enlisted and officer personnel to the organization and production responsibilities of the defense industrial base—is a clear indication that the entire establishment was in disarray.

The views in this essay are those of the author and not to be construed as those of The National War College, the National Defense University, the Department of Defense, or any other agency of the United States government.

What I shall attempt in this very tentative appraisal is to indicate where I believe the reforms have been successful and where there are major weaknesses. I shall not measure the reforms against another defense establishment, such as that of the United States, but against the weaknesses defined by the Chinese themselves.

I must also present a caution to the reader. This analysis is a function of reading what Chinese analysts and reporters write and of discussions I have had with various Chinese officers, officials, and scholars. The appraisal on the following pages is not the result of careful, empirical evaluation of China's military reforms. It is the result of indirect observation and therefore subject to considerable error.

Defense Reform and Modernization

The process of defense modernization was viewed by Deng Xiaoping in very broad terms and recognized as a complex, multi-faceted process. From its formal initiation in 1978 as the fourth of the Four Modernizations, the "modernization of national defense" was to have two very broad objectives. In the short term, it was to improve the current combat effectiveness of the Chinese armed forces. In the long term, it was to create a self-sustaining defense *establishment* capable of building and maintaining modern military forces and sustaining their requirements for technologically advanced weapons and equipment without excessive dependence on foreign suppliers.[1] In short, the goal was—and remains—to build the defense establishment required for a major power in world politics.

This was the same goal set in the early 1950s, when China, with massive Soviet assistance, set about building a defense industrial base capable of supplying its armed forces with equipment and armaments that extended from trucks and pistols to intercontinental ballistic missiles (ICBMs).[2] Similarly, Soviet military assistance teams trained Chinese troops in modern tactics and operations, while many officers went to the U.S.S.R. for professional military education and training. The Chinese political and military leadership, however, learned a hard and bitter lesson

106

in 1959 when the U.S.S.R. terminated its assistance to Beijing's nuclear weapons program and in the summer of 1960 terminated all civil and military assistance programs. The break came without warning and threw China's defense industries into chaos. It was not until 1965 that the defense industries began the series production of many of the weapon platforms and systems supplied by the U.S.S.R. Soviet technicians had departed taking their blueprints with them, and in many cases the machine tools to build advanced weapons had not been delivered. Chinese engineers had to go through the difficult and time-consuming task of designing the tooling by reverse-engineering tools from parts supplied as kits from which the Chinese were learning how to build the weapons and equipment.

The withdrawal of Soviet engineers and technicians was equally damaging to China's military modernization. Short of engineers and trained technicians, Beijing had to establish priorities for the weapons it was to design and build without Soviet assistance. The decision was to devote the majority of its limited technological resources to the nuclear weapons and ballistic missile program. As a consequence, weapons and equipment for China's conventional general purpose forces suffered.

These factors, when combined with the intensive involvement of the military in China's internal politics over the years 1964 to 1976, meant that by the mid-1970s the Chinese People's Liberation Army (PLA)—as the armed forces are collectively entitled—had become an aging, obsolescent giant incapable of conducting modern warfare.[3]

In 1978, when Deng began the process of defense modernization, it was clearly understood that the path ahead would be difficult to tread and would involve disputes over the allocation of resources, disagreement over the doctrine and strategy to guide the modernization of the armed forces, and considerable resistance from those officers who had developed a stake in the positions they had gained through years of political involvement.[4]

It must also be recognized that defense modernization was not undertaken as a response to a particular military "threat." Although the U.S.S.R. was clearly at the center of Chinese threat perceptions and was the measure against which short-term *military* modernization would be evaluated, the quasi-alliance with the United States was seen as at least a partial deterrent against a massive Soviet assault on China. Defense modernization was viewed by Deng then as it is now: as part of a broad pattern of national development designed to transform China into a major world power. Initially this transformation was to be completed by the year 2000. This ambitious goal was later more realistically set for the middle of the 21st century.

Thus, defense modernization was viewed as occurring in balance with the development of all other aspects of China's modernization objectives—in particular, that the defense industrial base would be modernized as part of the overall development of the civil industrial base. Indeed, the defense industrial base built since 1950, especially its expansion in the 1960s, was viewed as exceeding defense needs and wasteful of China's limited engineering and technological resources. The defense industries have therefore been required since 1984 to consolidate and contribute to the civil sector of the economy. Indeed, what we have been able to observe is a transformation of China's defense industrial base.[5]

Although this essay will divide its analysis into the two categories of short-term and long-term objectives for defense modernization, it should not be assumed that they are entirely separate and serial processes. They are, on the contrary, both related to one another and conducted simultaneously. There was also an apparent assumption on the part of China's decisionmakers that the two objectives would ultimately meld together at some undetermined future time.

The Short-term Objective: Improving Combat Effectiveness

The modernization of weapons and equipment was recognized as but one part of the complex process of modernizing the armed forces. Recruitment and training of both officers and enlisted men had to be radically changed, and tactical training of the conventional forces had to be extensively modified to reflect the demands of combat on the modern battlefield. Changes in military technology created battlefields where the speed and lethality of combined arms warfare blended with contemporary command, control, communications, and intelligence (C3I) capabilities and aroused the Chinese military's sensitivity not only to tactical requirements, but also to the absolute requirement for the logistical support essential to sustain forces in intensive combat. China's technologically backward combat aircraft, artillery, armored fighting vehicles (AFV), and naval combatants had to be properly employed and supported if they were to make the best possible use of their capabilities. To do this, however, required not only a well-trained officer corps and enlisted personnel, it also required a complete revamping of tactics, concepts of operations, and the organizational requirements for modern combined arms warfare.

Professional Military Education and Training[6]

Since 1979, the armed forces have sought to correct one of their basic problems: the lack of experience and understanding by their commanders in the intricacies of planning and employing the various Services in combined arms operations. To do so required major modifications in the recruitment, training, and promotion of its officers. In the past, officer candidates were selected from the ranks of young men and women who had shown promise while serving as enlisted personnel during their period of conscripted service. Beginning in the early 1980s, officers were recruited primarily from among college graduates and graduates of the 100 or so technical academies and schools specifically created to train a new generation of officers. Those recruited from the enlisted ranks must attend "command" schools prior to their commissioning and receive college degrees upon graduation. The revised promotion system also required attendance at the appropriate professional military education (PME) schools prior to promotion.

Such a radical change did not occur without considerable resistance, especially from the older generation of officers who had won their commands in the 1930s and 1940s. Ultimately, the generation of officers too old to function effectively on active service, especially those unable or unwilling to adjust to the education and training required of the new officer corps, were required to retire. Of the approximately one million soldiers who retired as part of a massive reduction in force (RIF), which was finally instituted after great difficulty between 1985 and 1987, some 600,000 were "cadres" or officers. As a symbol of the new officer corps, the ranks and insignia removed from the armed forces in 1965 were restored in 1987.

While a new, younger, and better educated officer corps was being developed, the education requirements for conscripted and volunteer enlisted personnel were increased. Men and women from urban areas were required to have completed middle school (high school), while those from rural areas had to be junior high school graduates. While officer candidates would still be recruited from the enlisted ranks, the development of a noncommissioned officer (NCO) corps was undertaken along with appropriate education centers.

The organization and training of the armed forces went under a similar radical change.[7] Prior to initiating these changes in 1979, Chinese officers and Services did not train as combined arms forces. The Chinese ground forces, once divided into field armies based upon light infantry divisions with only limited armor and artillery support, were formed into group armies fully integrating infantry, armor, field artillery, anti-aircraft artillery (AAA) and surface-to-air missile (SAM) batteries. Chinese officers' command experience, once limited to light infantry tactics with little use of AFVs, artillery, or airpower were introduced to combined arms warfare where the combat power of all Services and arms were integrated.

Such changes could not occur immediately but were introduced over the years in the early to mid-1980s. Use of combat aircraft for close air support and battlefield interdiction was especially difficult, requiring intense training of pilots and a complete revamping of the way in which both ground force and Air Force officers thought about and planned for combat operations. In the mid-1980s, special training areas were built specifically designed to allow the exercise of ground and air units in combined arms warfare.[8]

Combined arms exercises were only part of the revolutionary changes underway. In 1982, two exercises were conducted in northern China that simulated the use of tactical nuclear weapons. Clearly designed to defend against a Soviet attack in which the enemy forces used battlefield nuclear weapons to breach Chinese defenses, air-mobile forces were dropped into defensive positions while helicopters laid antitank mines to impede the enemy's advance.[9] In another exercise, Chinese forces south of the Mongolian People's Republic simulated the use of tactical nuclear weapons to break up a concentration of enemy forces. Close air support sorties, air-mobile forces employing helicopter assaults, and armored units were used to exploit the confusion created by the employment of nuclear weapons on the battlefield.[10]

Since these early years, combined arms training has become standard in Chinese military exercises. Officer training now includes planning for combined arms operations, including logistical support and intelligence preparation. There is constant reporting from China's PME centers that their curricula have expanded to include courses on nuclear deterrence, foreign military theorists, the history of warfare, electronic warfare, command courses utilizing computers to assist in battlefield decision making, and a variety of other courses all focused on understanding the complexities of modern warfare. It should be emphasized that, much like their Western counterparts, these schools also stress the study of classic military theorists in addition to Mao Zedong's military writings and Marxism-Leninism.

Of equal importance is the importance placed on the Chinese armed forces "opening to the world," or *kaifang*. Beginning in the mid-1980s, Chinese PME centers were increasingly open to foreign guests who lectured and conducted seminars for Chinese military students. The armed forces also sent their students and faculty abroad to study national security affairs, many coming to the United States.

Military Strategy and Operations

It is clear from the military exercises conducted by the Chinese armed forces, from the discussions and analyses found in Chinese journals specializing in military affairs, and from conversations with Chinese officers that there has been a radical change in the manner in which China plans to conduct military operations. By 1982, in their planning for a potential war with the Soviet Union, Chinese military operations had shifted from concepts based upon People's

War of the 1930s, which stressed "luring the enemy deep" and eroding his combat capabilities through attrition warfare. Between 1982 and 1985, it became evident from both theoretical analyses and field exercises that the goal was to mobilize quickly and conduct offensive operations early in the campaign. The military objective was to disrupt an attack and eject the enemy, thus limiting the damage inflicted by the enemy on China. Nuclear forces were to function both as a deterrent and as a potential battlefield capability if that should become necessary in war with a nuclear adversary.

In the spring of 1985, partly in response to the changing international environment but also to related changes in China's military capabilities, there was an important change in China's national military strategy. The Central Military Commission (CMC) declared that it was no longer necessary to prepare for an "early, major, and nuclear war."[11] While not stated, we may safely assume that China's previous military strategy was designed to deter a major war with the U.S.S.R. and to conduct such a war if deterrence should fail.

The new guidance from the CMC directed China's military strategists to prepare their armed forces for small-scale limited wars. What China faced, the CC guidance implied, was the possibility of small-scale wars erupting along its land and sea borders—including the remote possibility of limited war with the U.S.S.R. Chinese journals began to present a continuing series of theoretical analyses focused on the operational requirements of small-scale wars and unanticipated military crises involving only limited political objectives but requiring the swift and effective use of military forces.[12]

The year 1988 saw four large-scale military exercises designed to test the PLA's ability to conduct limited, but intensive, war. One was conducted in northwest China, another in northern China, and a third in northeast China. In each of these, the "enemy" was clearly the U.S.S.R. The fourth exercise was conducted in the South China Sea, where the presumed adversary had to be Vietnam. The exercises were designed to test the rapid deployment of Chinese armed forces for combined arms operations responding to "border clashes, accidents, and local warfare."[13]

Reviewing the reports of these exercises, they were clearly not designed to test the PLA's ability to conduct prolonged defensive war. The campaigns in northern China were designed to test the armed forces' ability in combined arms operations designed to disrupt and eject Soviet forces as early as possible. The exercise in the South China Sea was designed to test the PLA's capability in coastal defense and to defend territory it claims in the South China Sea.

The maneuvers all referred to the use of "special forces" as an integral component of the exercises. References to these forces began to appear in the mid-1980s, and they have played a prominent role in Chinese analyses of local war requirements. The size of these units is not known, but their mission requirements indicate they are probably small, well-trained combat units. They are trained to fulfill four major functions in an operation: as "door openers" striking at critical targets and widening a breach in the enemy's position; as a "scalpel" to strike at targets that when destroyed will paralyze an enemy's combat potential; as "steel hammers" to seize crucial enemy positions; and as "boosters" to speed up the tempo of an operation by opening up new battle areas within the invaded area.[14]

Forces with these roles are often referred to as "fist" (quantou) units and have been the focus of considerable discussion over the past seven years. Each of China's seven military regions (MR) has been reporting the development of "fist units" and rapid deployment forces designed to fit its own local situation and potential adversary. The PLA Marine Corps has received considerable publicity in these reports. Originally founded in 1953 but disbanded in 1957, the Marine Corps was reestablished on 5 May 1980 as the "fifth arm of the Navy." Headquartered at Zhanjiang, Guangzhou province, the Fleet Headquarters of the South Sea Fleet, the marines have received special attention as China's amphibious warfare forces clearly focused on the South China Sea.[15]

These units, however, perform an equally important function for the PLA's modernization process. As specially trained elite units designed for quick reaction in crises, they receive the very latest equipment. These units train with the equipment and gain experience in both tactics and in its maintenance. Given that these units are deployed in all seven MRs, new weapons and equipment are given field-testing in a variety of climates and units. The experience gained in tactical exercises and in field and depot maintenance is extremely valuable when these same weapons and equipment become more widely distributed as series production comes on line.

The Long-Term Objective: The Problem of Modern Armaments and Military Technology[16]

It was clearly recognized that the Chinese armed forces could not quickly upgrade their armaments. They were too large (approximately 3.2 million even after the 1985-87 RIF) and their needs were too great. Essentially all Chinese weapons and equipment were based on Soviet designs and technologies of the 1940s and 1950s. Air force combat aircraft were based on Soviet MiG-15/17/19/21 models. Chinese tanks were based on the T-54; field artillery and AAA and SAM systems were equally old. Naval surface and subsurface combatants were based on World War II or immediately post-World War II designs. Radars, communication systems, and other electronic systems were similarly outdated by the 1970s.

The choice made was to upgrade these systems primarily by retaining or marginally improving the weapon platform (tank, ship, aircraft, etc.) and improving the weapons and target acquisition systems employed by the platform. Arrangements were made with a number of foreign suppliers to undertake these projects. The United States, France, the United Kingdom, Italy, and Israel were all involved in a variety of different projects.

There was sound logic behind this procedure. First, the cost of obtaining sufficient and end-use items to reequip the entire army, navy, and air force would have been prohibitive. For example, the air force and naval air arm had between them some 5,000 fixed-wing combat aircraft, and the ground forces deployed some 12,000 tanks and many thousands of artillery pieces. Second, the task of developing the battlefield tactics, maintenance and support of armaments based upon advanced technologies would have overwhelmed Chinese capabilities. Finally, it would have been an

114

absolutely impossible task to train officers and enlisted personnel in the use of weapons and equipment that leapfrogged from 1940s and 1950s technologies into the 1970s and 1980s.

Taking armaments and equipment with which the Chinese armed forces had considerable experience and modernizing these systems in ways that improved their combat effectiveness without a major transformation of the platforms and the weapon systems was considerably more promising. Furthermore, as the modified systems were introduced to special units before their more universal deployment, those changes that were made could be better integrated into field units because the experience of these units could be used to ease the transition.

This process also fitted the long-term objective of defense modernization. It was not Deng's intent to rebuild the Chinese armed forces on the basis of purchased foreign weapons and equipment. A major objective of defense modernization is to build a research, development, testing, and evaluation (RDT&E) capability based upon an improved scientific and technological base (S&T) that will permit China to develop and produce its own weapons equipment. This process will be slow, for it is dependent on a number of factors. First, the number of scientists and engineers qualified to use and develop the most advanced technologies in electronics, materials and metals, etc., must be expanded. These skills are being acquired in the West. Military technology itself must also be acquired, both embedded in weapons and equipment and as items in themselves. These technologies are primarily found in the West, although electronic technologies are far more widely distributed. Then there is the problem of applying the technology with manufacturing methods, allowing series production of weapons and equipment that meet the stringent requirements for reliability under field and combat conditions. Once again, without experience in the series production of existing advanced technology weapons and equipment, it is unlikely that China will be able to develop the capabilities to design and produce their own systems.

There is now some evidence that in a limited number of areas China may well be achieving high levels of production sophistication. These areas include radars, surface-to-surface missiles using solid fuels at all ranges from battlefield to intercontinental targeting, cruise missiles, nuclear warheads, and other critical military capabilities. Some considerable progress may also have been made in nuclear power plants for submarines. Weaknesses are to be found in aircraft materials, high efficiency power plants for aircraft, gas-turbines for naval applications.

This potential progress notwithstanding, the armed forces have been extremely clear in their conviction that insufficient funding has been granted to reequip current forces with armaments sufficient for modern warfare. This complaint became especially vitriolic in the late 1980s. By this time, the armed forces had completed much of the reform initiatives undertaken in the late 1970s. The armed forces had been reorganized, the officer corps had been rebuilt with younger, better dedicated and trained officers assuming command at the Group Army-level and below. The concepts of operations that directed the battlefield tactics of armed forces had been radically changed. The training and field exercises of the armed forces had undergone dramatic change. For the military establishment, the greatest single drag on their combat capabilities was not the inability of the armed forces to properly employ high-technology weapons equipment. By the late 1980s, the military establishment was arguing that the greatest impediment to improving its combat capabilities was the state of its weapons and equipment.[17]

This demand for more rapid modernization of its armaments was made even more pressing, the military argued, by the nature of the war they were ordered to prepare for. War fought for limited political objectives in the current military environment requires quick and immediate action. Modern limited war is a far cry from people's war of the past, when the entire country was mobilized and the core of China's military strategy was based on time and attrition. The potential wars now facing China and the wars the Chinese armed forces are explicitly ordered to prepare for require quick, lethal military action. As military spokesmen have stated their dilemma, in the next war the first battle may well be the most crucial. The stunning success of American military technology in the 1991 Persian Gulf War provided yet another arrow to the PLA's quiver of defense budget demands.

Chinese military commanders do not expect technology to bring victory, but they now see their operational flexibility hindered by the technological limitations of their weapons and equipment. The "Desert Storm" campaign fought by the United States and its coalition allies is now seen by Chinese military leaders as the epitome of modern warfare. It was a war that contained the central characteristics of the conflicts they have been charged with preparing for since the spring of 1985. The war was unexpected; it was fought for limited political objectives; it was conducted as a combined arms campaign using all resources from space systems to riflemen; it was fought by extremely well-trained troops using high technology weapons and equipment; and it was fought with great speed and lethality. The Iraqi forces, using weapons and equipment that in many cases replicated those employed by Chinese forces today, could not provide effective resistance to the coalition's high technology warfare.

The increase in China's defense budgets from 1988 to 1992 reflected in part the leadership's recognition that the political crisis which surrounded the Tiananmen tragedy resulted in greater dependence on the armed forces. It also reflected a response to the military establishment's complaint that inflation had seriously eroded the purchasing power of their budget and was thus eating into the modernization program. The Gulf War only added impetus to the military's charge that modernization could not be effectively pursued with the meager funding it was receiving. The emerging "Russian connection" seen in the purchase of 26 Su-27s (F-15 equivalent) may well reflect the political leadership's decision to commit more funding to the purchase of both end-use items. It may also be the overt sign of a decision to purchase the licensed production of a wide range of Russian military equipment. If this is the case, then the vocal complaints of the military over the past few years that it needs advanced weapons and equipment now rather than in the distant future is receiving a sympathetic response. How far this will go is currently a matter of pure speculation.

A Tentative Appraisal

From the point of view expressed by China's military analysts, Deng's reforms have made less than satisfactory progress. Their complaint, however, reflects a specifically military response to a very complex development strategy. Deng did not intend to reform the Chinese defense establishment overnight. It must be recalled that Deng Xiaoping's conceptualization of defense modernization was as part of a national development program. Rather than seeking to bring the armed forces' combat capability up to the contemporary standards of the major industrial powers in a short period of time, Deng sought and continues to seek a defense capability that will serve China in the 21st century. The purchase of weapons and equipment that fulfill current needs does not serve the long-term strategic requirements Deng has in mind. There is, therefore, a tension between Deng's grand design and the need perceived by the armed forces for weapons and equipment that provide the combat capabilities they see required by the current security environment.

While this is an understandable tension, it must be clearly stated that my own assessment is not especially favorable toward the opinions expressed by the Chinese armed forces. Although I am not confident I can penetrate Deng Xiaoping's evaluation of China's current security environment, it would seem to be almost self-evident that China is militarily safer now than at any time since the Opium War of 1839–1842. The U.S.S.R. disintegrated, and the military threat to China's northern borders has dissolved. While it is understandable that China would keep a wary eye on developments within Russia, it is extremely unlikely that within the next decade any major military threat will reemerge from Russia. There is now no state that represents the kind of military threat that would require or impel Deng to retreat from his original design for defense modernization.

What is more, there is no state close to China that maintains the combination of quality and quantity in armaments requiring Beijing to plan for a war that would demand its armed forces to use massive amounts of high technology arms and equipment. Certainly China's soldiers are apprehensive about Japan's future policies as they look to the 21st century. There is even a certain amount of apprehension over India's future course. Nonetheless, it would take a major commitment to a worse case analysis to drastically modify Deng's strategy for defense modernization.

If I were to speculate on the potential for change in Deng's approach to defense modernization based upon an expansionist China, similar problems emerge. Even with all the speculation over the potential for a hot war over conflicting claims to the territories in the South China Sea, such a conflict would not require a massive employment of advanced weapons. Indeed, even if China were to purchase an aircraft carrier such as one of the Russian *Kiev*-class now being withdrawn from service in the Pacific Fleet, it would be at least five years before such a vessel could become an effective combatant in Chinese hands.

Indeed, I find it difficult to find any situation where it is plausible to anticipate a conflict where China would be at a major disadvantage because of weapons and equipment that are outdated by the standards of the advanced industrial powers. It is on this assumption that my assessment will be based.

The Strengths of Deng Xiaoping's Program

The primary strength of Deng's defense modernization strategy is that, if followed for a sufficient period of time, it will provide China the defense capability it needs to act as a major military power. If China can design and build its own weapons and equipment without undue reliance on foreign technology and suppliers, then it can have the confidence a major power requires to act independently in the international system. That capability will permit China to design a national military strategy and build and train a force structure to support that strategy without fear that foreign suppliers will undermine China's independence of action.

It is my judgment that Deng's approach to defense modernization as it has emerged over the past 14 years has been successful, and that if consistently followed, will achieve its long-term objective. Its achievements over the past 14 years are, at a minimum:

- A military leadership that, at the very highest levels, understands and supports policies that create a trained, technically proficient officer and NCO Corps.

- A rebuilt professional military education and training system capable of producing officers and military units competent in planning and conducting modern warfare.

- A logical support system that, although not fully competent in supporting modern warfare, is well aware of the weaknesses it must correct.

- Armed forces that, although still dominated by the ground forces, fully appreciate the need for combined arms warfare and the synergistic effect combined arms provide.

- A force structure well into the process of being rebuilt in order to respond more effectively to the demands of modern combined arms warfare.

- An S&T and RDT&E base that understands the need for cooperation across institutional boundaries and is developing the capability to design new weapons and equipment in selected high priority areas.

- A defense industrial base becoming more efficient in its use of resources and more competent in the series production of high technology weapons and equipment.

The Weaknesses in Deng Xiaoping's Program

The primary weakness of Deng's approach to defense modernization is that, until very recently, it may have been to willing to sacrifice current needs to better serve long-term objectives. This becomes important when it is recognized that military technology is a "moving train." Whereas it makes economic and strategic development sense to minimize the purchase of end-use items and military technologies that do not represent the cutting edge of capabilities, without some intermediate steps the armed forces may be facing too large a leap when they make the transition from their current equipment to the latest available. In short, China may well have reached the point where modifying current armaments and equipment produces results not worth the cost. The F-8 "Peace Pearl" project canceled by the Chinese may be an example of this dilemma.

In addition, the frustration felt by many senior officers as they develop concepts of operations that cannot be supported by their current armaments and are therefore required to modify these concepts, may significantly undermine the morale of officers at all levels. Although I hesitate to use the term *professionalism*, there is clearly a point where technically proficient officers at all grades become frustrated by a defense establishment that cannot, or will not, fulfill what they perceive as minimum military requirements.

The weaknesses in Deng's program appear to be:

- An officer corps with eroding morale that is losing confidence in a defense establishment that does not appear to be responsive to their needs as soldiers charged with defending China.

- An officer corps whose pay and allowances have not kept pace with the compensation available to other sectors of society with similar skills and less patriotic commitment to the nation.

- A force structure equipped with arms and equipment generations behind not only the leading industrial powers but also neighboring armed forces. Chinese officers are well aware that their forces deploy systems technologically far behind those of Japan and India and behind lesser powers such as Thailand, Malaysia, Singapore, and Indonesia.

- Weapons and equipment that lag significantly behind current military technology does not permit an easy transition to more advanced systems when they do become available.

Conclusion

It is more than possible that the emerging military technology relationship with Russia, and possibly other former Soviet republics such as Ukraine, is a response to the weaknesses in Deng's strategy for defense modernization.[18] Whereas the military reform and modernization program as it has emerged over the past 14 or so years is well suited to China's long-term development objectives, there have been some negative consequences. While not damaging to the development strategy itself or to China's national security, these negative effects are harming the morale of the new officer corps and creating potential difficulty in absorbing more modern arms and equipment as they become available in the future. Thus, the purchase of end-use items and the potential for licensed production of Russian arms and equipment could well fulfill multiple needs and represent an adjustment in Deng's strategy for modernizing China's national defense.

Such an adjustment could have been forced on Deng by the reality that the use of the armed forces to violently quell the demonstrators in and around Tiananmen Square had a severe impact on the morale of the armed forces, especially the officer corps. The substantial erosion in the officer corps' morale was simply compounded by the consequences of defense budgets that did not keep pace with inflation.[19] The standard of living of officers and enlisted ranks eroded even as military modernization was retarded by insufficient funding. The consequence of these factors was a severe reduction in morale and a probable tendency for younger officers to leave the armed forces in search of greater rewards in China's growing market economy.

If this interpretation is correct, then what we are observing is a mid-course correction perhaps typical of Deng's pragmatic response to reform and modernization. There is no reason that defense modernization should be any less subject to Deng's pragmatism than any other aspect of his strategy for China's long-term development.

ENDNOTES

1. For a more detailed discussion of the logic and processes of China's military reform program, see Paul H. B. Godwin, "The Chinese Defense Establishment in Transition: The Passing of a Revolutionary Army?" in A. Doak Barnett and Ralph Clough (eds.), *Modernizing China: Post-Mao Reform and Development* (Boulder and London: Westview Press, 1986), 63-80.

2. For useful discussions of Soviet assistance programs, see Raymond I. Garthoff, "Sino-Soviet Military Relations," *The Annals of the American Academy of Political and Social Science*, September 1963; and J. G. Godaire, "Communist China's Defense Establishment: Some Implications," Congress of the United States, Joint Economic Committee, *An Economic Profile of Mainland China* (Washington, D.C.: United States Government Printing Office, 1967).

3. Deng Xiaoping, "Speech at an Enlarged Meeting of the Military Commission of the Party Central Committee" (14 July 1975), in *Deng Xiaoping Wenxuan* (Selected Works of Deng Xiaoping) (Peking: 1 July 1983) in Joint Publications Research Service, *China Report* (hereafter JPRS-China), 31 October 1983, 19.

4. Paul H. B. Godwin, "Changing Concepts of Doctrine, Strategy and Operations in the Chinese People's Liberation Army 1978-87," *The China Quarterly*, no. 112 (December 1987): 572-590.

5. For a detailed analysis of this transformation, see Paul Humes Folta, *From Swords to Plowshares? Defense Industrial Reform in the PRC* (Boulder: Westview Press, 1992).

6. William R. Heaton and Charles D. Lovejoy, "The Reform of Military Education in China," in Charles D. Lovejoy, Jr., and Bruce W. Watson (eds.), *China's Military Reforms: International and Domestic Implications* (Boulder and London: Westview Press, 1986), 91-100; and Godwin, "The Chinese Defense Establishment," 69-71.

7. See, for example, Ellis Joffe, *The Chinese Army After Mao* (Cambridge, Mass.: The Harvard University Press, 1987), 69-71.

8. Beijing, Xinhua, 22 April 1986, in *Foreign Broadcast Information Service, Daily Report: People's Republic of China* (hereafter FBIS-China), 24 April 1986, K9.

9. Peking, Xinhua (New China News Agency), 20 July 1982, in FBIS-China, 22 July 1982, K2-4.

10. *Ningxia Ribao* (Ningxia Daily), 27 June 1982, in FBIS-China, 6 July 1982, K19-20.

11. See Generals Zhang Zhen and Li Desheng's discussion of the CC's guidance at a meeting with the editorial board of *Jiefangjun Bao* (Liberation Army Daily), reported in *Ta kung pao* (Hong Kong), 16 February 1986, in FBIS-China, 18 February 1986, W11-12.

12. Paul H. B. Godwin, "Chinese Military Strategy Revised: Local and Limited War," *The Annals of the American Academy of Political and Social Science* (January 1992), 191-201.

13. Xu Jingyao, "1988: A Year of Reform for the Chinese Army," *Liaowang* (Overseas edition, Hong Kong), no. 3, 16 January 1989, in FBIS-China, 24 January 1989, 36.

14. Liu Qianyuan, "A Cursory Analysis of the Characteristics of Limited War of the Future," *Jiefangjun Bao*, 19 December 1986, in JPRS-China, 23 September 1987, 91.

15. Deng Huaxu and Li Daoming, "A Visit to the PLA Marine Corps," *Renmin Ribao* (People's Daily), Overseas edition, 2 August 1988, in FBIS-China, 3 August 1988, 30–31.

16. For a very useful analysis of Chinese policy in this area, see Wendy Frieman, "Foreign Technology and Chinese Modernization," in Lovejoy and Watson, *China's Military Reforms*, 51–68.

17. See, for example, Wang Chenghan, "On Coordinated Development of National Defense and the Economy," in *Hongqi* (Red Flag), 1 September 1987, in JPRS-China Report, 7 December 1987, 18. This essay in what was until 1989 the Communist party's most authoritative journal is but one of many essays over the past decade stressing the need to modernize the armed forces weapons and equipment.

18. Mr. Yeltsin's public commitment during his mid-December visit to Beijing to sell to China Russia's most advanced military technology, when combined with earlier sales and frequent exchanges of high-level military officers, may signify the formation of a major Sino-Russian military cooperation program. See Lena Sun, "Russia, China Set Closest Ties in Years," *Washington Post*, 19 December 1992, 10.

19. Directorate of Intelligence, *The Chinese Economy in 1991 and 1992: Pressure to Revisit Reform Mounts* (Washington, D.C.: Central Intelligence Agency, July 1992), 12.

CHAPTER SIX

China in World Affairs Under Deng Xiaoping—Background, Prospects, and Implications for the United States[*]

ROBERT G. SUTTER

Overview

Some of the most notable achievements in Chinese foreign policy have come under the leadership of Deng Xiaoping. In assessing the accomplishments and setbacks in China's approach under Deng's leadership, it is necessary first to emphasize the positive. In particular, China today faces no major strategic threat for the first time since the establishment of the PRC. While China's policies under Deng's leadership were not central to the collapse of the Soviet Union and the demise of the Cold War, the Chinese government under Deng was effective in safeguarding China's basic national security interests in the face of sometimes serious threat, especially from the U.S.S.R. Also, China today has managed to establish cordial or workman-like relations with all countries throughout its periphery—an accomplishment unprecedented in the history of the PRC. Meanwhile, Chinese leaders have

---

[*]*The views in this chapter are the author's and not necessarily those of the Congressional Research Service, The Library of Congress.*

used China's location, economic reform policies, and other advantages to place China in a seemingly advantageous position for further growth and development in East Asia, the most economically dynamic area of its size in the world.

To be balanced, a review also needs to note some of the problems and difficulties facing Beijing. The Communist leadership has been discredited to some degree by its handling of dissent at the time of the Tiananmen demonstrations in 1989 and by the collapse of Communist regimes in much of the rest of the world. Many in China and abroad believe that it is only a matter of time for Beijing's Communist system to pass away. Thus, the Communist government currently faces the most serious threat to its political legitimacy. In Asia, too, China faces problems as many in China believe that Beijing's influence in the region should be greater as both Russia and the United States withdraw; they fear the rising power of Japan and possible coalitions of other powers (for example, ASEAN and Indochina) to "fill the vacuum" and to block the expansion of Chinese influence. And, although China's economic prospects look reasonably good, Beijing's political future appears tenuous to many who warn of political succession struggles and difficulties associated with political decision making in a time of rapid economic and international change.

Given the current fluid atmosphere in East Asia, it seems timely to review Chinese foreign policy and assess its status and prospects. In the United States, meanwhile, there is considerable debate over China's foreign approach and its implications for the United States. Some journalistic accounts stress a growing capability and tendency on the part of Chinese leaders to disrupt the Asian and world environment in ways contrary to American interests. They warn in often alarming terms of China's alleged plans to purchase weapons, expand military activity, and promote policies abroad contrary to U.S. interests. Thus, a balanced assessment of China's role in the world also could conceivably assist in the U.S. policy debate regarding China.

As it stands now in the U.S. policy debate, Americans arguing in favor of a relatively moderate and closely engaged U.S. policy toward China tend to highlight in their often balanced assessments of China's policy the ample evidence of China's pragmatism in world affairs, including Chinese willingness to respond to calls by the United States and others for China to change policies in areas where Chinese behavior is seen as antagonistic to U.S. interests. Proponents of a tougher, more assertive U.S. policy toward China than has prevailed in recent years argue that Chinese pragmatism is limited, and they focus on numerous areas of Sino-U.S. friction where the PRC appears unwilling to change unless pressed much harder by the United States.

Recent trends and likely prospects in Chinese behavior in world affairs and in how Chinese behavior affects current American security, economic, and political interests may on balance favor those Americans arguing for a tougher, more assertive approach to China than has prevailed in the past few years. Of course, a case is made by advocates of a more moderate U.S. approach that China's proven record in the past two decades is one that shows remarkable progress toward relative pragmatism, moderation, and general support for the status quo in world affairs, and that it is in the interest of the United States to further encourage Chinese behavior along lines advantageous to the United States. The best way to do so, in their judgment, is to reciprocate Chinese moderation while working with China to modify areas of continued differences. In contrast, proponents of a tougher, more assertive U.S. policy toward China point to many areas of Sino-American differences despite the relative pragmatism and moderation in China's recent foreign policy.

The latter had the upper hand in the U.S. policy debate in large measure because the political calculus in the United States over China policy had changed markedly after the June 1989 Tiananmen incident and the end of the Cold War. U.S. politicians generally have been more inclined than in the past to criticize and pressure China. They have been influenced by the Tiananmen Square crackdown, the collapse of the U.S.S.R., and the focus on negative features of Chinese behavior for U.S. interests on the part of the media, interest groups, and others. They no longer have followed the practice of the previous two decades when U.S. leaders endeavored to soft pedal differences with China while successfully emphasizing positive features of U.S.-China policy (for example, cooperation against the U.S.S.R).

Ironically, China's relatively moderate and pragmatic approach to world affairs has strengthened the U.S. tendency to press China. In particular, it has weakened the warnings of those Americans who have advised against a tougher U.S. approach on grounds that it could prompt a sharp Chinese reaction contrary to American interests. The development of Chinese practice in world affairs over the past 20 years has shown that any such sharp shift away from recent practice is likely to hurt China's interests more than it does the United States.

As it turned out, the Clinton administration took power on the basis of a policy platform strongly critical of the Bush administration's "soft" policy toward China. The new administration's subsequent rhetoric and actions were more balanced, however, with the president notably reaching a compromise with important congressional leaders that was tougher than President Bush's stance but was successful in preserving growing U.S.-Chinese economic and other relations.

Introduction

Since the June 1989 Chinese government crackdown on anti-government demonstrations at Tiananmen Square and other locations and the 1991 demise of the Soviet Union and end of the Cold War, U.S. China policy has changed markedly:[1]

- Close high-level U.S.-PRC leadership collaboration against Soviet expansion and in support of Asian stability has sharply declined as senior U.S. leaders refrain from close association with their Chinese counterparts;

- U.S. willingness to cut back ties with Taiwan for the sake of improved ties with Beijing has been replaced by a more supportive U.S. stance toward Taiwan, even on such sensitive issues as sales of advanced U.S. jet fighters and entry into international governmental organizations;

- U.S. practice to play down disputes over unfair or unscrupulous Chinese trade and weapons proliferation policies has given way to the strongly assertive U.S. stance on both issue areas seen today;

• U.S. government support for collaborative intellectual-cultural programs has declined as advocates for a more assertive effort to convey American values to China via a U.S.-funded surrogate radio station gain strength; and

• U.S. efforts to handle human rights issues through a long-term process of encouraging reform while dealing with specific cases through diplomatic channels has given way to the much more assertive U.S. stance on human rights, self-determination, and democratization regarding Chinese dissidents, Tibet, and Hong Kong, among other issue areas.

The change in U.S. policy has not been smooth. An important debate, viewed in simple terms, continued between an approach favored by the Bush administration, which approach supported relatively moderate and continued close U.S. interaction with China, and a more assertive approach, favored by many in Congress, which argued for greater U.S. government pressure against China in the interest of preserving and enhancing American values and other concerns in relations with China. The Clinton administration eased this debate by successfully reaching in mid-1993 a working consensus among U.S.-China policymakers in the executive and legislative branches, while placing limited conditions on renewal of U.S. most-favored-nation (MFN) tariff treatment for Chinese imports. Nevertheless, the U.S. debate over China policy continued and a major element in that debate has related to China's behavior in the world. In general, the debate treats China's behavior in the world in two ways:

• Advocates of the relatively moderate approach tend to emphasize in their often balanced assessments the positive importance of China's role for U.S. interests and stress China's willingness to respond to the calls of the United States and others for China to change policies in areas where Chinese behavior is seen as incompatible

131

with U.S. interests. By contrast, advocates of a more assertive approach emphasize the negative impact of Chinese behavior on U.S. interests and stress China's reluctance—unless pressed hard by the United States and others—to change policies in areas of U.S.-PRC incompatibility.

• Advocates of the more moderate and balanced approach tend to emphasize U.S. interaction and engagement with China and warn that the United States pressing China hard on sensitive issues could lead to negative consequences, including Chinese actions in world affairs with serious consequences for U.S. interests. Advocates of an assertive U.S. policy stance focus on the utility of heavy U.S. pressure and counter fears over adverse consequences from U.S. pressure with the argument that such pressure is unlikely to lead to Chinese policy behavior any worse than in the recent past.[2]

Congress continues to play an important role in promoting change in U.S.-China policy. Members of Congress have been in the lead in prodding the administration to adopt more assertive and sharply defined approaches in defense of newly prominent U.S. interests regarding China, involving such fields as human rights, arms proliferation, and trade equity. Others in Congress have seen wisdom in the administration's more balanced, moderate approach toward the PRC.

This paper provides context, perspectives, and a comprehensive assessment regarding issues related to China's behavior in the world. Specifically, the paper:

• describes the major features of recent Chinese government actions in world affairs, explaining their background, status, and prospects;

• examines how those actions affect U.S. interests; and

- assesses how Chinese actions in world affairs support or detract from the respective approaches adopted by Americans in the current debate over China's policy.

China in World Affairs Prior to the Tiananmen Crackdown[3]

Under the leadership of Mao Zedong, China was capable of wide swings in foreign policy behavior. During the 1950s, Mao charted a pro-Soviet, anti-U.S. foreign approach; in the 1960s, China shifted to a posture antagonistic to both superpowers; and in the 1970s, Mao sanctioned a realigning of China toward a rapprochement with the United States in opposition to perceived Soviet expansion. Throughout this period, Chinese leaders under Mao mixed hard and soft tactics in foreign affairs in ways that showed a strong willingness to threaten or use force in order to seek advantage or to respond to perceived encroachment or pressure from outside. China cultivated the image of a "have not" power determined to struggle to change the world—at least over a period of time. Beijing supported revolutionary political movements and gave arms and training to radical insurgencies directed against established governments.

Outside analysts were able to discern core goals in Chinese foreign policy notably involving support for the security of the Chinese state and its Communist party leadership; development of China's wealth and power; and China's strong desire to stand strong and independent in world affairs. Nevertheless, the frequent shifts in priorities and tactics have often caught Chinese leaders unaware or unresponsive, leading to leadership confusion and conflict. Also, domestic politics would sometimes spill over into Chinese foreign policy, leading to sometimes serious leadership foreign policy debates. Perhaps the most graphic example of the latter occurred in the mid-late 1960s, during the most violent phase of the Cultural Revolution. This period saw a collapse of Chinese foreign policy, amid a broader collapse of Chinese government and party institutions, reflecting the life-and-death struggle for power then underway among the senior leaders in China.

The internal chaos of this stage of the Cultural Revolution was matched by the bankruptcy of Maoism in foreign affairs. Chinese stridency had alienated Beijing from most foreign support while placing it in direct opposition to the United States, then deepening its military involvement in Indochina and the U.S.S.R., which was then building its military power along China's northern border as a defense and possible lever to press China. The 1969 Sino-Soviet border conflicts brought China to the brink. Chinese security was more endangered than at any time since the Korean War and arguably since the establishment of the PRC.

Adroitly maneuvering to save China in this time of danger, while saving himself from leadership adversaries who ultimately perished in the struggle for power at this time, Premier Zhou Enlai and close associates laid out and followed a more pragmatic, less ideologically driven plan for Chinese foreign policy. Subsequent leaders, notably Deng Xiaoping, established pragmatic domestic development strategies that served to reinforce the trend toward relative pragmatism, moderation, and continuity in Chinese foreign policy behavior.

Evolution of Chinese Policy Since the Cultural Revolution

China's relationship with the superpowers and especially the Soviet Union remained at the heart of Chinese foreign policy through much of this period. In particular, Soviet power and influence repeatedly got in the way of China's efforts to expand its influence in Asian and world affairs, as part of Chinese efforts to seek broad foreign policy goals of security, independence, and development. Of course, developments in China and other international trends also helped to determine China's policy approach. In general, Chinese foreign policy went through four distinct phases from 1969 to 1989.[4] They are briefly described as follows:

1969-1976. During this period, China was only beginning to emerge from the violent domestic conflict and international isolation caused by the Cultural Revolution. The Soviet military buildup and the Sino-Soviet border clashes prompted a major reassessment in Chinese foreign policy that focused on countering the Soviet threat to Chinese security. As the United States was pulling back militarily from Asia under terms of the Nixon doctrine, Beijing saw an opportunity to work with this former adversary against Soviet pressure in Asia. The result was an agreement in the Shanghai communiqué signed during President Nixon's visit to China in 1972 that both sides opposed the efforts of a unnamed third party (presumably in the U.S.S.R.) to establish "hegemony" in Asia. Subsequently, Beijing broadened the scope of this understanding to encourage worldwide efforts to block the expansion of what China called "Soviet hegemonism." China was sharply critical of any moves by the United States or others that it perceived as efforts to accommodate Soviet expansion.

China was generally supportive of the gradual U.S. withdrawal from Vietnam set under terms of the Paris peace accord signed in January 1973, but it was alarmed by the rapid collapse of pro-U.S. regimes in South Vietnam and Cambodia in 1975. Beijing saw a particular danger that expanding Soviet power and a unified Vietnam would fill the power vacuum left by the United States. Chinese pronouncements encouraged the United States to remain actively involved militarily, economically, and politically in Asia and pointedly warned Asian countries to beware of Soviet efforts to fill the vacuum created by the U.S. pullback.

The basis of the Sino-U.S. accommodations that emerged during this period was restricted largely to strategic factors. Because of ongoing leadership struggles, China remained unwilling to break away from Maoist development policies emphasizing Chinese "self-reliance." China also remained very cautious in developing educational, cultural, and technical contacts with the outside world that might be called into question by the ideologically rigid members of the so-called gang of four—Maoist radicals who had significant influence over policy at this time.

1976–1980. This period began with the death of Mao, the purge of the Maoist "gang of four," and the rehabilitation of more pragmatic leaders led by Deng Xiaoping. Deng and his reform-minded colleagues began a major economic and political reform effort designed to end the ideological struggles of the past and to improve the material well-being of the Chinese people.[5] In foreign affairs, they broadened the basis of China's interest in contacts with the West and the rest of the developed world from continued common anti-Soviet strategic concerns to include greater economic, technical, and other exchanges.

Chinese foreign policy supported China's new quest to achieve economic modernization as effectively as possible. It did so by helping to promote economic contacts with various countries that could benefit China's modernization and by helping to maintain a stable and secure environment in Asian and world affairs that was conducive to Chinese modernization efforts. In this context, Chinese leaders put aside ideological and other constraints to beneficial economic and technical interchange with a wide range of developed and developing countries. They halted to cut back support to Maoist insurgents or political groups that would impede smooth economic exchanges abroad; cut back sharply on Chinese foreign assistance to the Third World; and showed an increased willingness to soft-pedal past Maoist pretensions to change the world.

Chinese leaders focused their foreign policy concerns on establishing a "peaceful environment" around China's periphery in Asia. China did not control the environment, which remained more heavily influenced by the Soviet Union, the United States, their allies, and associates. China continued to see the main danger of instability and adverse development in Asia coming from the Soviet Union or its allies and associates. Thus, Beijing was particularly concerned by the Soviet-Vietnamese strategic alignment that allowed Vietnam in late 1978 to invade Cambodia, overthrow the Chinese-backed Khmer Rouge regime there, and successfully resist the subsequent Chinese military incursion into Vietnam. Although the Soviet Union did not respond in kind to the Chinese incursion, it beefed up military and economic support for hits Vietnamese ally and made substantial military countermoves along the Sino-Soviet border, including the largest military exercise ever seen in the region since World War II.

The economic and strategic imperatives noted above underlay China's decision to normalize diplomatic relations with the United States in 1978; the signing of the China-Japan peace treaty in 1978;

and China's highly vocal effort at this time to encourage a worldwide "anti-hegemony front" to contain the expansion of the Soviet Union and its proxies in Asia and elsewhere in the Third World. As it was in the previous period, Beijing was especially critical of perceived efforts by the United States or others in the West to accommodate or "appease" perceived Soviet or Soviet-backed expansion in the interest of U.S.-Soviet arms control or other concerns. It was also supportive of a continued strong effort by the United States and its allies to maintain a firm military and diplomatic position against Soviet expansion in Asia and elsewhere.

1981-1984. Chinese leaders were generally pleased by the strong U.S.-led international response to the Soviet invasion of Afghanistan in December 1979. China did its part by providing support to the Afghan rebels along with continued Chinese support to the anti-Soviet, anti-Vietnamese resistance in Cambodia. The election of Ronald Reagan and the buildup of U.S. military strength in the early 1980s were seen by Beijing as complementing similarly strong efforts against Soviet expansion by U.S. allies in Europe and Asia. As a result, China came to view Soviet expansion as held in check for the first time in over a decade—a trend that Beijing judged was likely to continue to pose difficulties for a U.S.S.R. leadership already preoccupied with problems, including leadership succession and deepening economic malaise.

Meanwhile, Chinese leaders began to reassess their close alignment with the United States in light of candidate Reagan's strong statements of support for Taiwan. In response, Beijing opted for a more "independent" posture in foreign affairs that struck a favorable political chord in China and among Third World countries deemed important to China.

Leonid Brezhnev and subsequent Soviet leaders attempted to exploit Sino-U.S. frictions over Taiwan and other issues and to make a breakthrough in Sino-Soviet relations. But they were unwilling to compromise in reducing Moscow's military forces around China's periphery or in reducing support for Asian countries, like Vietnam and India, that served as local counterweights to Chinese influence. Moreover, Chinese leaders also clearly recognized the importance of their newly developed economic ties with the United States, Japan, and other Western-aligned countries. As a result, after two years of tough negotiations and public disputes with the Reagan administration over U.S. arms sales to Taiwan and other issues, Chinese leaders set limits on China's independent foreign posture, compromised on heretofore sensitive bilateral disputes with the United States, and consolidated ties with the United States during President Reagan's visit to China in 1984. The Reagan administration facilitated this change by increasing the flow of U.S. technology to China and by soft-pedaling public references to differences with Beijing over Taiwan and other issues.

1985-1989. With the rise of Mikhail Gorbachev and his reform-minded colleagues in the Soviet Union, China and the Soviet Union moderated past differences and appeared determined to improve political, economic, and other relations. Leaders of both sides focused on problems of internal economic development and related political reform, and both were interested in fostering a stable, peaceful international environment conducive to such reform. Sino-Soviet ideological, territorial, and leadership differences of the past were less important. The two sides remained divided largely over competing security interests in Asia. Gorbachev began to meet Chinese interests in this area by starting to pull back Soviet forces from Afghanistan, Mongolia, and other places around China's periphery in Asia. As a result, Chinese military planners began to revise substantially China's strategic plans, downgrading the danger of Soviet attack and allowing for a major demobilization of Chinese ground forces.

The Soviet initiatives also dulled Chinese incentive to cooperate closely with the United States and its allies and associates in Asia to check possible Soviet expansion or for other reasons. China's growing need for close economic and technical ties with these countries compensated to some degree for the decline in Chinese incentive for closer security ties with them. Nevertheless, China was less inclined than in the previous periods to side with the United States and its allies in opposition to Soviet policy in Asia, and it was less supportive of sensitive U.S.-allied military arrangements focused against the U.S.S.R.

Chinese leaders also wished to improve relations with the Soviets in order to keep pace with the rapid improvement of Gorbachev's relations with the United States and Western Europe. Otherwise, Chinese leaders ran the risk of not being considered when world powers decided international issues important to China. As a case in point, some reports said that Chinese leaders were upset by the absence of a significant Chinese role in negotiations leading to the Soviet military withdrawal from Afghanistan—an area important to China. Beijing was said to be determined to avoid such an eventuality in dealing with the Vietnamese withdrawal from Cambodia.

The United States and its allies also found the Soviet Union more accommodating of Western interests, and they were able to make greater progress than in the past in dealing with issues affecting Western security concerns. In particular, Gorbachev made a series of accommodating decisions affecting Western security concerns over Intermediate Nuclear Forces (INF), conventional force deployments in Europe and Asia, and Soviet forces in Afghanistan. The change in Soviet policy thereby reduced the perceived U.S. need to sustain and develop close strategic cooperation with China against the U.S.S.R. Many analysts also judged that the United States saw that economic interchange with China was of insufficient importance to compensate for the reduced strategic cooperation. As a result, longstanding bilateral and other irritants in U.S.-China relations over human rights, treatment of intellectuals, and Tibet appeared to take on more prominence in Sino-U.S. relations.[6]

Results

Several significant trends emerged from the development of Chinese foreign policy over this 20-year period.

1.   Chinese leaders now saw the security environment around China's periphery as less likely to be disrupted by a major international power than at any time in the past. Of course, the reduced big power military threat did not preclude danger posed by possible conflicts between

China and its neighbors over territorial disputes or other issues, which China itself might have provoked. Nor did it automatically translate into growing Chinese influence in Asia or sanguine Chinese leadership attitudes regarding the evolving balance of influence in Asia. Regional economic and military powers (for example, Japan, Indonesia, India) were among leaders asserting their influence as East-West and Sino-Soviet tensions subsided.

2. Regional security trends were generally compatible with China's primary concern with internal economic modernization and political stability. So long as the regional power balance remained stable and broadly favorable to Chinese interests, Beijing seemed likely to continue to give the pragmatic development of advantageous economic contacts top priority in its foreign affairs.

3. Ideological and leadership disputes had less importance for Chinese foreign policy than in the past. Although Chinese leaders could be divided between more conservative-minded officials and those who are more reform-minded, the differences within the leadership over foreign affairs appeared markedly less than they were 20 years earlier.

4. Reinforcing the more narrow range of foreign policy choices present among Chinese leaders, Chinese foreign policy had become more economically dependent on other countries, especially the Western-aligned, developed countries, than in the past. Particularly as a result of the new openness to foreign economic contacts and the putting aside of Maoist policies of economic self-reliance, Beijing had come to see its well-being as more closely tied to continued good relations with important developed countries, notably Japan and the United States. They provided the assistance, technology,

investment, and markets China needed to modernize effectively.

5. China's overall pragmatic adjustments to world affairs were not dependent on just one or two leaders in China. Although Deng Xiaoping picked up senior foreign policy-making duties from Mao Zedong and Zhou Enlai, the policies followed represented, in broad terms, a consensus among senior Chinese leaders who were advised and influenced by a wide range of experts and interest groups in China. Many of these groups had a strong interest in dealing pragmatically with world affairs. This included particularly strong economic, technological, and other interconnections between Chinese enterprises and interest groups and counterparts outside of China. As a result, they were loathe to pursue autarchic, contrary, or provocative policies that would jeopardize their particular concerns as well as China's economic progress in an increasingly interdependent world.

Recent Foreign Policy Challenges—Beijing's Response[7]

The sharp international reaction to China's harsh crackdown on dissent after Tiananmen caught China by surprise. Chinese leaders reportedly had expected developed countries to move more swiftly back to China after a few months, but they had not counted on the rapid collapse of communism in Eastern Europe and the subsequent march toward self-determination and democratization throughout the Soviet empire, leading to the end of the U.S.S.R. by 1991. This unexpected turn of events not only diverted the developed countries from returning to China with advantageous investment, assistance, and economic exchange, it posed the most serious challenge to the legitimacy of the Chinese Communist regime since the Cultural Revolution.

In response, Beijing endeavored in foreign affairs to demonstrate to skeptical audiences at home and abroad the legitimacy and prestige of its Communist leaders. As time went on,

Chinese leaders managed to reestablish a modicum of political stability, although deep fissures and competing leadership ambitions lay below the surface and occasionally were reflected in strong debates in the official media. Open factional fighting, social turmoil, and economic collapse predicted by some did not come to pass, however. After a few months following the Tiananmen incident, Beijing managed to avoid further excesses in economic or political retrenchment and maintained an approach to foreign affairs that avoided taking egregious action in economic and other areas that would jeopardize the pragmatic interests of the Chinese state.

Global trends caused serious anxiety and ambivalence among Chinese leaders, who have remained uncertain as to what recent trends really mean for Chinese interests and what China should do about them. On the one hand, Chinese leaders recognized that the Tiananmen massacre repelled many in the developed world, while the collapse of the U.S.S.R. sharply reduced China's strategic importance to these countries. Beijing was particularly concerned that new international emphasis on democratization, human rights, and self-determination could challenge and undermine the legitimacy of the Chinese Communist regime. On the other hand, Asian states tended to respond more moderately to the excesses of Tiananmen, and the collapse of the U.S.S.R. created a power vacuum providing China with more strategic freedom of movement in Asia than at any time in the past. The attraction of continued impressive economic growth in China proved important to Asian and developed countries interested in capitalizing on economic opportunities at a time of lackluster economic performance in many other parts of the world.[8]

In this fluid situation, Chinese leaders have demonstrated a range of often competing views on global trends and what they meant for Chinese interests.[9]

    a)   *China as a balancer*–Reflecting a strongly economic determinist way of thinking, along the lines of Marx and Lenin, Chinese leaders sometimes express optimism that the apparent unity among developed countries will soon pass as economic frictions and competition will divide the

United States from Japan and the European Community. Under these circumstances, a new "balance of power" will emerge where China presumably would be in a more advantageous position than it is today, as each of these protagonists sought Chinese support in their competition for economic dominance.

b)   *China faces a unipolar world*—This view sees China facing a difficult situation at least for some time. For the time being, only the United States is seen to have the broad range of political, economic and military power capable of leading world affairs; economic strongholds Japan and Germany are vexed by historical and other complications that check their overall power and cause them to follow along with the United States. In so far as the United States makes the changing of China's Communist system and other Chinese domestic and foreign practices an issue between Washington and Beijing, the Chinese leaders are caught in a dilemma of, on the one hand, not wishing to confront the powerful United States and, on the other, not wishing to give ground in areas that would challenge the legitimacy and staying power of the Communist regime.[10]

c)   *China in an interdependent world*—This view sees China (as well as the United States and other states) caught up in a web of economic and other interdependencies that make unilateral action difficult and often counter-productive. The United States needs to accommodate the views of its allies and associates; America remains dependent on world economic trends. These and other interdependencies mean that a strong U.S.-led effort to press for the overthrow of China's leadership appears unlikely. China is too important to the world's political, economic, and security conditions to be treated in such a way. China too needs to accommodate wherever possible transnational and other world trends that affect its development and well-being. On this basis, the United

States and China can seek common ground and work together to assure mutual advantage.[11]

Regarding *Asian Affairs*, Chinese leaders appear to have achieved greater consensus and the record of Chinese achievement is more impressive. Whether Chinese leaders believe that the United States and others in the West are determined to work with Beijing in an interdependent world or to press for the overthrow of the Communist regime, Beijing is likely to follow a similar approach to Asian issues; that is, in either case China is likely to see distinct advantages in improved relations with the countries throughout its periphery. Such improvement will serve to broaden China's constructive relations with an interdependent world, or it will help set up a ring of protection of nearby countries against the possible pressures from nations further away.

The collapse of the Soviet empire has prompted several important Asian states previously close to the U.S.S.R. (for example, Vietnam, Mongolia, India) to adjust policies in a more forthcoming way toward China, and Beijing has reciprocated with enthusiasm. China has also endeavored to develop advantageous economic, political, and cultural ties with the newly independent Central Asian republics. Beijing continues longer standing efforts to develop positive economic, political, and military ties with non-Communist Asian states.

Despite its obvious success in broadening diplomatic relations and economic ties amidst the most favorable strategic situation around China's periphery since the establishment of the PRC, Chinese leaders still show signs of being anxious about the current situation. At bottom, this angst appears to reflect the realization that China did not determine the forces that led to the recent favorable changes. Far more important was the collapse of the U.S.S.R. and the resulting changes in the balance of influence in Asia.

Thus, Chinese officials worry that the situation could change again. For instance, although many in China fear U.S. intentions, many also are concerned that the United States could pull back further from Asia, resulting in a power vacuum possibly dominated by Japan. At least some in China are sensitive to the fact that non-

Communist countries along China's periphery might become so alarmed by PRC military modernization as to lead to a de facto alignment against perceived PRC expansion and power. To preclude such unwanted outcomes, Beijing has worked hard to expand its influence in the region, using the wide array of political, economic, and military tools available. On occasion, Chinese efforts appear to work at cross-purposes, as they have done in the recent controversy over the Spratly Islands in the South China Sea. In such cases, Chinese diplomats have attempted to reassure others in the area, including countries with which Beijing recently opened diplomatic relations, but this has been seen as at odds with the assertive Chinese naval patrolling and territorial claims, backed by a well-publicized buildup of Chinese air and naval power in the area.[12]

Internal Trends saw Chinese leaders briefly revert to a policy after the Tiananmen incident that was designed to limit the influx of ideas and influences from abroad in the interests of preserving and insulating the Communist system from outside influences. The result was a strong effort to reassert administrative control of the economy that succeeded in lowering inflation but sharpened economic inefficiencies by favoring the poorest industrial performers at the expense of the more competitive industrial enterprises. Stagnant growth, declining government revenues, and political pressures from constituencies representing more competitive enterprises prompted Chinese leaders to put aside the policy of control in favor of policies stressing ever greater economic interaction with the outside world. The rationale of this approach, graphically underlined during Deng Xiaoping's widely publicized inspection tours in early 1992, stressed that China's Communist system would almost certainly be overthrown if it continued to squelch prospective economic growth in the interest of maintaining political control. A better strategy focused on using the advantageous wealth created through ever-expanding economic interchange with the world to deal with the perceived negative influences that enter China through the ever-widening "open door."[13]

Prospects

From one perspective a review of Chinese behavior in world affairs reflects a trend toward relative pragmatism and moderation that is designed to support Chinese leaders endeavoring to build the wealth and power of the Chinese state in a more or less conventional fashion. Others would tend to emphasize continued and possibly recently increasing signs of Chinese interest in military expansion and other Chinese inclinations opposed to U.S. interests, even though Beijing has become more pragmatic in various areas of foreign affairs over the past 20 years. Whether one can expect trends toward more or less pragmatism and moderation in China's behavior over the next few years depends on two sets of factors:

1. Internal—political stability and the course of economic and political performance;

2. External—the interaction of Chinese relations with key states around its periphery and Chinese adjustment to international trends in the so-called new world order.

Internal Stability and Reform

China's continued preoccupation with internal economic and political developments is likely to support pragmatic trends in China's foreign policy and exert a generally positive, stabilizing influence on Asian and world affairs. Some observers are concerned, though, that China may change course during the 1990s. A change in domestic policy could lead to a turn toward a more assertive and potentially destabilizing posture. It could involve stronger Chinese efforts to spread weapons of mass destruction to unstable states in regions of vital world importance like the Middle East. It could involve strong support for insurgencies or mobilization of Chinese military power, especially China's growing naval and air forces, in an effort to use force or threaten to use force to intimidate nearby smaller states. It is noteworthy that officials and other observers from the countries of Southeast Asia and elsewhere in the region often privately and sometimes publicly

146

express apprehension about a more assertive Chinese policy affecting them in the 1990s.

Developments inside China that could cause such a change in policy are:

- a major economic failure or change in political leadership that would prompt Beijing leaders to put aside their current approach to nation-building in favor of a more assertive foreign policy; this could be accompanied by harsher reactions to internal dissent and to Western influence in China;

- the achievement of such a high level of economic success and social-political stability that Chinese leaders would feel confident that China was strong enough to pursue its interests in the region and elsewhere with less regard for the reaction or concerns of other countries.

It might be good for Asian and world stability if China continued to make progress toward economic modernization, but failed to achieve rapid success. Under these circumstances, Beijing leaders would likely continue to see their interests as best served by pursuing a moderate, conventional nation-building program. They would likely remain preoccupied with the difficulties of internal modernization and would not achieve the level of success that would allow for a more forceful policy in Asian and world affairs for some time to come.

In fact, an examination of variables governing China's development and reform efforts shows that Beijing appears to face just such future prospects. Beijing leaders are unlikely to achieve fully their current development objectives until well into the 1990s, if then, because of significant economic constraints, the complications from efforts to implement proposed reforms, and leadership and political instability. Major short-term economic constraints include an inadequate transportation system, insufficient supplies of electric power, an expanding government spending deficit, money-losing state enterprises, and not enough trained personnel. Long-term impediments include growing population

147

pressure, the difficulty of obtaining enough capital to develop available energy resources and general industry, and the slowdown of agricultural growth after the rapid advances in the recent past.[14]

Reflecting these and other important constraints, the Chinese leadership at present continues to delay some changes in prices because it fears they would have serious consequences for Chinese internal stability. Such changes can trigger inflation and cause hoarding. Closing inefficient factories forces workers to change jobs and perhaps remain unemployed for a time. Decentralized economic decision making means that local managers can use their increased power for personal benefit as well as for the common good. The result of these kinds of impediments has been a zig-zag pattern of forward movement and slowdown in economic reforms.

The problems of political stability focus on leadership succession and the difficulty Beijing has in trying to control students, workers, and others demanding greater accountability, less corruption, or other steps that would curb central authority. The repeated political difficulties over the results of the economic reforms and political measures continue to demonstrate the volatility of politics in China.

Of course, the widely publicized difficulties of the reform efforts sometimes obscure their major accomplishments and the political support that lies behind them. Reflecting the rapid economic growth in China over the past 15 years, the constituency favoring economic reform includes representatives of coastal provinces, enterprise managers, prospering farmers, many intellectuals, and technically competent party officials. The major alternatives to current policies (for example, Maoist self reliance, Soviet-style central planning) have been tried in the past and have been found wanting. Some of the followers of purged party leader Zhao Ziyang provided an alternative favoring greater political as well as economic reform, but thus far no leader has emerged with a viable program or constituency able to lead China in a direction markedly different than the current Communist party-led development effort. Thus, on balance, it appears likely that Beijing will remain focused on economic reform and related political change, even in the event of strong leadership and political disputes and economic complications in the next few years. From one view,

China's continued preoccupation with such internal developments will support recent trends in Chinese foreign policy and exert a generally positive, stabilizing influence on Asian and world affairs, although others stress concern about what they see as Chinese assertiveness in the post-Cold War order in Asia.

External Relations[15]

The Former Soviet Union

The military threat posed by China by the Soviet Union was downgraded substantially by PRC leaders in the 1980s and is now not of major immediate importance. Indeed, at no time in the past has the PRC been so free from great power military pressure and threat. Russia, the newly emerging central Asian countries, and the new Mongolia do not pose a substantial national security threat to China over the near term. Beijing can relax its military guard against them.

Instability in these areas could pose a danger to China's desire to maintain firm control of minority populated areas along the inland frontier of China. The collapse of communism in the U.S.S.R. has also put pressure on PRC leaders to justify their continued efforts to legitimate the Chinese Communist party as one of the few remaining ruling Communist parties in the world. Meanwhile, the attention of developed countries has focused heavily on events in the former Soviet empire, diverting resources of these countries from China to help bring about a transition to non-Communist political, economic, and social systems in the former Soviet bloc.

The United States

Although the United States does not border on China, actions of the United States and the course of China's relations with the United States have an important bearing on China's policy in Asia. Beijing recognizes that the United States still exerts predominant strategic influence in East Asia and the Western Pacific; is a leading economic power in the region, surpassed only by Japan; and is one of only two world powers capable of exerting sufficient power around China's periphery to pose a tangible danger to Chinese security and development. As the world's only superpower, the United States also exerts strong political influence, to a degree that Chinese Communist leaders play up signs of U.S. approval (leadership visits, etc.) as signs adding legitimacy to Chinese Communist rule.

With the end of the Cold War and collapse of world communism, U.S. foreign policy is in transition and subject to debate.[16] Viewed in simple terms, the debate can be seen to focus on three tendencies or schools of thoughts. Some see an interdependent world in which the United States must work constructively with major world actors, including China, in seeking solutions for serious world problems or preservation of important U.S. interests abroad. Others see U.S. involvement abroad as generally working against American interests. They call on U.S. leaders to "come home," to focus on rebuilding U.S. economic, technological, and social strengths that have been depleted in the pursuit of U.S. leadership in world affairs. A third tendency stresses the opportunity posed by current circumstances. It stresses the need for the United States to pursue a vigorous American agenda in world affairs, encouraging the development of democracy, free market enterprise, and other features of the U.S. political, social, and economic system. The outcome of the United States policy debate remains unclear. It is possible that the United States could come up with policy approaches that would prompt a strong Chinese reaction that would result in a substantial shift in China's recent, generally pragmatic approach to foreign affairs.

Seen below are some U.S. measures that some believe could prompt a significant reassessment and possible change in China's current approach to Asian and world affairs. The chances of the United States adopting these measures seem uncertain.[17]

- United States withdrawal of an active military presence in the region. This could happen in conjunction with a U.S. withdrawal from the bases in the Philippines or other circumstances. It could force Beijing to reassess its security position vis-à-vis other perceived security concerns in the region.

* U.S. measures designed to reduce sharply access to U.S. markets or technology by China and perhaps other newly industrializing Asian nations. Such restrictions could prompt Beijing to reassess the importance it now places on smooth economic interaction with the United States and other developed non-Communist countries.

* U.S. efforts to encourage separatist-minded opposition politicians in Taiwan to move toward independence; strong U.S. efforts to promote political democracy and free enterprise in the China mainland; or U.S. efforts to build through diplomatic, military, or other channels mechanisms to press for change in China and curb the perceived expansive tendencies of China's Communist leaders. Such approaches could represent a serious challenge to the Chinese Communist leadership's sense of national unity and development and prompt a major reassessment by Chinese leaders of the pros and cons of smooth U.S.-Chinese relations.

Japan, Korea[18]

China's relations with Japan and Korea likely will continue to reflect the delicate balance of often conflicting economic and security concerns. Japan seems likely to follow policies over the next few years conducive to China's continued preoccupation with economic development. Thus, the Japanese appear to continue to rely on the United States for security support and to use their economic might and slowly growing military power to support greater economic development and peace in Asia. Japan remains China's major source of foreign assistance and advanced technical equipment.

As part of its more relaxed stance regarding Soviet policy in Asia, Beijing muted or reversed past vocal support for greater Japanese defense efforts, the U.S.-Japan security treaty, and the U.S. military presence in Japan. It also muffled public support for

151

Japanese claims to the so-called Northern Territories, islands north of Hokkaido that have been occupied by Moscow since World War II.

Indeed, as the perceived danger of Soviet military expansion subsided, some official Chinese pronouncements and popular demonstrations registered sharply critical views of Japan's growing role in Asian affairs. Some warned bluntly about the danger of revived Japanese militarism; criticized U.S. encouragement of greater Japanese military spending; and sharply attacked alleged Japanese efforts to "infiltrate, control and exploit" the Chinese and other Asian economies. Other, more sophisticated Chinese views also registered concerns over alleged expanding Japanese efforts to use economic-backed power to gain political and economic influence in parts of Asia considered sensitive by China. In particular, some Chinese officials have expressed concern that Japan may use improved trade and aid relations with Vietnam, Laos, and Cambodia to build strong influence there once the war in Cambodia is settled. At bottom, however, Chinese leaders have been loathe to allow such concerns to interfere substantially with China's interest in encouraging greater trade, investment, and assistance from Japan.[19]

In Korea, Beijing has worked since the mid-1980s to reduce tensions associated with the dangerously volatile military confrontation between North Korea and U.S.-backed South Korea. It has seen the tense arms race on the peninsula working against Chinese interests. Thus, in the 1980s the U.S.S.R. used its ability to provide advanced fighter aircraft and other equipment China could not provide in order to gain greater influence in Pyongyang. Military confrontation also increased the risk of a conflict that could pit China (an ally of North Korea) against its main economic partners in the United States and Japan (supporters of South Korea). The North-South split in turn slowed Chinese efforts to open greater economic exchanges with economically dynamic South Korea. China made considerable progress in trade relations with South Korea. The $5.8 billion annual trade represents several times the value of China's trade with North Korea. Beijing hesitated to move faster in exchange with South Korea for fear of alienating North Korea. The Chinese are especially sensitive since North

Korea's leader Kim Il-Song is aged, has groomed his reportedly unstable son for what is likely to be an uncertain political succession, and is trying to develop weapons of mass destruction, notably an atomic bomb. Nevertheless, China and South Korea announced the establishment of diplomatic relations on 24 August 1992.

Over the longer term, some Chinese observers worry about the implications of Korean reunification. Some see a reunified Korea as a hedge against emerging Japanese power, but others worry about scenarios in which Japan would come to dominate the peninsula in opposition to China's influence there. They also worry about the economic and security challenges a reunified, possibly nuclear-armed Korea would pose in its own right.

Taiwan, Hong Kong[20]

Beijing's main political concern regarding Taiwan has been to check the possible emergence of "separatist" political tendencies on the island that would challenge the long-standing position of "one China" held by the Communists on the mainland and the Nationalists on Taiwan. At present, movement toward *de jure* political independence on Taiwan is held in check by Nationalist leaders in Taipei who continue to adhere to the "one China" principle for practical and ideological reasons and by the growth in trade and people-to-people contacts between the island and the mainland since 1987, when Taipei dropped formal opposition to Taiwan residents visiting the mainland for family reunions and other humanitarian reasons.

Beijing's concerns about separatist trends on Taiwan are not unfounded. Taiwan's rapidly growing economy has pushed per capita income to $10,000 a year—contrasted with a level of under $500 per capita on the mainland. The recent relaxation of authoritarian political and other controls in Taiwan stands in contrast to Beijing's crackdown on political and intellectual dissent. The opposition party in Taiwan advocates the right of the people of Taiwan to determine their political future—including political independence. (The party's stance enjoys some support from U.S.

officials in Congress, although the Bush administration repeatedly affirms its support for "one China.")

The Nationalist leaders in Taiwan have begun to modify their past rigid adherence to their claim of being leaders of the legitimate government of all of China. Under the rubric of "flexible diplomacy," they now publicly discuss possible diplomatic arrangements that would continue to recognize the principle of "one China" but would also recognize that there are two competing governments in China. This "one China—two governments" or "one China—two areas" stance has been condemned by Beijing officials as an effort to garner international recognition of Taiwan's separate identity from the mainland.

Beijing's concerns over Taiwan are linked to its management of the return of Hong Kong to Chinese sovereignty in 1997. Beijing has held up the "one country—two systems" model it created in the 1984 Sino-British agreement calling for Hong Kong's reversion as a model for Taiwan's reunification with the mainland. The credibility of Beijing's promise to allow autonomy in Hong Kong after 1997 plummeted as a result of its handling of student-led demonstrators in China in mid-1989. It was unclear what the longer-term effects of the crisis would be on the stability and prosperity of Hong Kong, although the economy in Hong Kong improved by the early 1990s. If Beijing grossly mismanages the Hong Kong situation, resistance in Taiwan to any sort of union with the mainland could grow. Beijing also has an important economic stake in Hong Kong, which is China's main trading partner and its main source of foreign exchange and investment. Although there is more uncertainty than ever as to what Hong Kong residents will do as 1997 approaches, one view among those who plan to stay in the territory after reversion appears to be a wish to avoid confrontation with Beijing. These individuals appear determined to make the best of the situation by encouraging Beijing to see that China's interests are served best by leaving Hong Kong with as much autonomy as possible.

Indochina, Southeast Asia[21]

As the Vietnamese withdrew forces from Cambodia in the late 1980s, China focused strong efforts to insure that a peace agreement in Cambodia would guarantee complete Vietnamese military withdrawal and the establishment of a new government in Phnom Penh that was not dominated by the Vietnamese. The collapse of the U.S.S.R. increased Vietnamese incentives to accommodate China over Cambodia and other disputes, and China was ready to reciprocate in the interests of securing its southern boundary and playing a prominent role in the Cambodian settlement. Beijing now seems prepared to pressure its client, the Khmer Rouge, as they threaten to disrupt the Cambodian settlement process, which China sees as serving its interests in securing influence in Indochina and elsewhere in Southeast Asia.

There remains a risk that some other power or coalition of countries will emerge to challenge and resist Chinese interests in Southeast Asia. Japan is one possibility. At present, Beijing seems to anticipate that there will be a number of regional and other powers active in the region but in ways that do not fundamentally challenge Chinese interests. One area of possible exception involves the conflicting territorial claims of China and Southeast Asian nations to islands in the South China Sea. There, assertive Chinese military actions have appeared to belie Chinese diplomats' expressions designed to reassure Southeast Asian nations of Chinese intentions. China has also worked with U.S. oil companies to assert its claims to resources under the sea. An intensified territorial dispute might cause the ASEAN states to seek greater outside support against China, setting the stage for a confrontation in the region.[22]

South, Southwest Asia[23]

Elsewhere in Asia, China is likely to be an important foreign policy player, but it remains hampered by distance and geographic barriers from exerting as strong an influence as it does in Northeast and Southeast Asia. In South Asia, India's ambition and defense

155

buildup support its ability to face China along the disputed border. The two sides, however, have downplayed tensions, and relations have improved, especially since Prime Minister Gandhi visited Beijing in December 1988—the first high-level state visit since the Sino-Indian border war 30 years earlier.

India depended heavily on the Soviet Union for advanced military equipment. Now it needs to find other suppliers. India also seeks to reach out to China, Japan, the United States, and the West as it readjusts its foreign and domestic policies to take account of recent world trends. While China is prepared to reciprocate Indian gestures of good will, it continues to supply Pakistan, India's main strategic rival on the subcontinent, with an array of aircraft, tanks, and other military equipment.

Beijing has used arms sales and transfers of sensitive technology to gain economic profits and garner influence throughout the Persian Gulf region. China has sold several billion dollars worth of arms to Iran, Iraq, and Saudi Arabia. Its influence suffered a setback after the 1990-91 Persian Gulf War, but Beijing has worked hard to reestablish strong ties with Iran and others in the region during the ensuing period. Recent Sino-Iranian exchanges reportedly include the sale of a small Chinese nuclear reactor to Iran. Nevertheless, few world conflicts lent themselves as readily to Chinese weapons sales, and Chinese transfers declined sharply by 1990-91.[24]

Features of the New World Order: Implications for China's Policy

Whether or not there is continued pragmatism in Chinese foreign policy will also depend on transnational issues and trends and how they could possibly affect China. In general, those features often reinforce trends supporting continued Chinese pragmatism in world affairs, or they have results that are less than probable to result in consequences that would see a substantial shift in Chinese policy.[25]

The international, western-led norms of the new world order include:

a) **Greater emphasis on international organizations, especially the United Nations.** This trend seems to work to the advantage of China's current policies. It assures that China, by virtue of its seat on the Security Council, will continue to play a major role in world decisions. Other powers that might be inclined to pressure China will need to take account of China's U.N. role in assessing their policies.

b) **International trade practices.** The developed countries and the financial institutions they lead are requiring countries like China to adhere more closely to free market and less politically controlled economic development approaches. This puts pressure on China's desire to follow certain neo-mercantilist strategies in order to build foreign exchange reserves to purchase needed commodities, including high technology, abroad. While Chinese leaders might be expected to resist outside pressures for more reform and transparency in the Chinese economy, they also want to maintain access to foreign markets in order to gain foreign exchange and purchase high technology.

c) **Arms transfers and proliferation.** Recently enhanced international efforts to curb the sale of weapons systems and technology associated with weapons of mass destruction pose a direct concern to segments of the PLA and others in the Chinese leadership. They rely on these sales for their personal benefit and to gain the foreign exchange needed to purchase needed technology and supplies abroad. The sales also build better political relations as well as other ties where China's military can possibly gain access to information, technology, and other material that developed countries try to restrict in transfers to China.

One can argue that China's leaders are prepared to adjust to this feature of the new world order, even though on balance it probably has a more negative than positive impact on immediate Chinese interests. Longer term Chinese interests may be seen as better served by preserving an image of Chinese cooperativeness with international regimes to control the proliferation of sensitive weapons systems and technologies. A case can be made that the actual lost sales for China from such control regimes may be small, while the intangible but substantial costs of China appearing to obstruct global arms control would appear large. Of course, China will almost certainly try to have its cake and eat it too (for example, appear cooperative but also engage in sales where possible). In any event, the sharp decline in Chinese arms sales in recent years—due largely to market forces—suggests that this issue may be less important in determining Chinese policy in the future;

d) **Drugs, terrorism, environment.** Beijing has appeared generally cooperative in working with recently enhanced international efforts to curb the flow of drugs, to pressure those who harbor terrorists, and to deal with worldwide environmental issues. Significantly, such cooperation involves infringement on traditional Chinese concepts of national sovereignty, but Beijing has gone along with international efforts in these areas with little complaint and often with considerable enthusiasm. Evidently, Chinese leaders bridle at some outside "intrusions" into China's or other countries' sovereign affairs (for example, over human rights issues—see below), while they wink at others;

e) **Human rights.** China seems to take particular offense with heightened world efforts to press China to bring its human rights practices into closer alignment with the broad participatory, accountability and democratic standards followed by other governments. It sees such pressure as an affront to China's national sovereignty and as designed, at bottom, to undermine the legitimacy and power of the Chinese Communist regime. Beijing is particularly concerned when human rights issues are used in conjunction with calls for greater freedom for self-determination in places like Tibet and Taiwan. Such outside advocacy is then seen to amount to little more than disguised efforts to overthrow China's government and split the nation apart.

Chinese leaders are especially concerned about this aspect of the new world order. Nonetheless, a pragmatic Chinese approach is still warranted if one judges that the ability of outside powers to threaten China is limited. Limits are imposed by distance, the absence of major resources devoted to this effort, and major differences in the West and among Asian-Pacific countries regarding how prominent a role human rights should play in their interactions with a country like China.

Implications for U.S. Interests[26]

For two decades, China's behavior in world affairs was seen on balance to favor American interests. During the 1970s, U.S. policymakers tended to highlight the role China played in support of U.S. strategic interests vis-à-vis the Soviet Union and in maintaining a favorable balance of influence in Asia, as the United States withdrew over 600,000 forces from Indochina and elsewhere in East Asia. Sino-U.S. trade grew from a small base and was generally favorable to U.S. exporters of grain, aircraft, and other products. There were pointed differences in the United States over China's repressive Communist system and its support for some insurgents, and other practices abroad, but those differences in values and other areas were often overshadowed by the emphasis on common U.S.-Chinese efforts to support world peace (for example, to contain the power of an expanding Soviet empire). President Nixon's landmark visit to China in 1972 set a pattern that showed American politicians how to use visits to China and interchange with senior Chinese leaders to benefit their standing in American domestic politics.

In the 1980s, there was a broader base of Sino-American commonality. China's economic and political reforms were added to China's continued strategic importance for U.S. interests in balancing Soviet power, preserving peace and fostering development in Asian and world affairs. The Chinese reform efforts were important in easing the U.S. debate over close interaction with the Chinese Communist system. It was now commonly argued that the U.S. interaction served to promote further reform, thereby leading to the ultimate transformation of the Communist regime. As a result, U.S. values of democracy, human rights, and free-market enterprise were often seen as well served by the direction of Chinese reform, even though it was quietly acknowledged that China had "a long way to go." By combining these perceived advantages for U.S. interests with the more long-standing U.S.-Chinese effort to promote world peace and stability, U.S. politicians used close interchange with Chinese leaders to advance their stature in American politics. Thus, President Carter cited his normalization with China as one of his major accomplishments during the 1980 presidential campaign, while President Reagan used adroit scheduling and travel planning to garner over one week of favorable front-page coverage devoted to his China trip in the period leading to the 1980 presidential election campaign.

Since the reassessment of U.S.-China policy following the Tiananmen crackdown and the end of the Cold War, Chinese behavior in world affairs is seen to provide more negative or mixed results for U.S. interests. In many cases, the implications of Chinese behavior for U.S. interests are a matter of debate. In general, those favoring a balanced and moderate U.S. engagement with China argue that Chinese behavior tends to support U.S. interests, while those favoring greater U.S. pressure stress the contradictions between Chinese actions and U.S. policy concerns.

Security Interests

China's role as a counterweight to the U.S.S.R. has fundamentally changed. The United States no longer worries very much over the need to build international coalitions to defend against Soviet expansionism. China continues to play an important role in promoting stability and sustaining a favorable balance of influence in Asia (for example, Korea and Cambodia). But the positive U.S. view of China's role in this regard has changed somewhat as U.S. officials have found they can work directly with former adversaries (e.g., Russia) and that former regional antagonists (e.g., North Korea, Vietnam) are especially solicitous of improving relations with the United States. Under these circumstances, Americans view in a somewhat harsher light those aspects of Chinese behavior in the region that do not appear to support directly U.S. interests. These include aspects of China's support for North Korea, the Khmer Rouge, and the military regime in Burma; Chinese diplomatic and military assertiveness over disputed territories in the South China Sea; and China's resistance to U.S.-backed efforts to have Japan play a larger, more responsible political-military role in Asian and world affairs.

Regarding international organizations and some of the newly salient global issues of the new world order (for example, proliferation, trade practices, environment) the Chinese record is subject to mixed reviews. U.S. supporters of a more balanced and moderate U.S. posture toward China acknowledge some Chinese deceit but tend to emphasize China cooperativeness and accommodation to U.S. and other international concerns. U.S. critics stress perceived shortcomings that see Chinese representatives abstain on important U.S. Security Council votes, fail to follow-up with meaningful measures regarding Chinese pronouncements of support for programs on global issues of importance to the United States, or withdraw from international forums on important global issues out of anger over U.S. behavior toward China.

Economic Interests

China is viewed as both an opportunity and a problem as far as U.S. economic interests are concerned. The Chinese economy is growing steadily and is becoming increasingly integrated with other East Asian economies—the most dynamic area of economic opportunity in the world in the early 1990s. China's need for investment, technology, equipment, and materials provide great incentives for American entrepreneurs. The negative features of Chinese behavior center on Chinese unfair trading practices that result in a rapidly growing bilateral U.S. trade surplus with the United States. Americans wanting to pursue a moderate engaged policy with China tend to argue that the Chinese are coming to terms with international trading norms, whereas critics tend to stress the need for strong U.S. pressure in order to change Chinese behavior antithetical to U.S. interests.[27]

Values

Prevalent U.S. media coverage tends to see Chinese behavior as contrary to American values. This is due partly to the fact that the media in recent years has focused heavily on individual rights and democracy. Chinese behavior in these areas is widely seen as contrary to American interests and Chinese leaders are often viewed as unwilling or unable to take meaningful steps to bring Chinese practices more into line with U.S. or other internationally accepted practices.

The picture for American interests is more mixed when one adds American values regarding human material welfare, development, and world peace. In these areas, Chinese leaders perform in ways generally seen as compatible with American interests, although this compatibility is not often brought to the attention of U.S. policymakers or the American public. For example, the massive Chinese relief effort following major flooding in the Yangtze Valley over the last year dealt effectively with tens of millions of affected people without placing a burden on already overworked international relief agencies. China's economic development practices assure that the vast majority of people in China have access to the basic necessities of life and the likelihood of a better material life in the years to come. Because of China's massive population and underdeveloped economic infrastructure, a major failure in the Chinese economy or negligent government practices could result in disastrous costs in human sufferings, deaths, and massive flows of refugees.

Domestic Politics

It is in the area of U.S. domestic politics where the U.S. view of China in the world (as well as other features of China's behavior) has undergone the greatest change in recent years. The prevailing emphasis on negative features of Chinese behavior in the U.S. media by various interest groups pressing for changes in Chinese practices and in the often acrimonious debate in Washington over U.S.-China policy has reinforced the changed calculus among U.S. politicians about close interchange with China. The pattern of the Nixon, Carter, and Reagan years no longer prevails. Close interaction and association with Chinese leaders are now seen as something to be avoided rather than to be sought after. Although the analysis of China's behavior in world affairs noted above shows a mixed picture as far as U.S. security, economics, and values are concerned, in U.S. domestic politics, assessments of Chinese behavior in this and other policy areas emphasize the negative. Thus, negative features of Chinese behavior are highlighted and used to strengthen arguments that pose serious political risks for U.S. politicians who might want to promote or become more closely associated with a more balanced, moderate posture intended to improve U.S.-PRC relations.

Implications for U.S. Policy

A case can be made that Chinese behavior in world affairs shows enough compatibility with current U.S. interests to warrant a more moderate, accommodating, and engaged U.S. policy toward China. Such a U.S. stance could be justified on the basis of common U.S.-Chinese concerns and practices regarding Asian stability and development, global proliferation, environmental issues, international economic issues, and the advancement of human material progress in the Third World. As the United States and others effectively engage with Chinese leaders in a series of bilateral and multilateral forums on issues of mutual concern, it can be said that Beijing would likely accommodate more prevailing trends and further mute points of difference important to the United States. China's recent willingness to accommodate international concerns on arms proliferation and U.N. peacemaking are all cases in point. American leaders also could point to the argument that close, balanced U.S. engagement helps economic progress that inevitably will lead to political, social, and other changes that will force adjustments in China's Communist system leading either to its transformation or demise.

On the other hand, an examination of China's record and its implications for U.S. interests may be more likely to strengthen—at least over the short-term—the hands of those Americans who argue for stronger U.S. efforts to press for change in Chinese behavior. There remain plenty of examples of Chinese practices that are not generally compatible with American interests and where U.S. leaders presumably could argue for stronger pressure for change in Chinese behavior. Perhaps of more importance, these examples continue to feed a political calculus in the United States that makes it difficult for politicians to advocate a more moderate approach to China. To do so is to run against a tide of commentary in the media, among interest groups, and in Congress that emphasizes the negative in China and supports a tougher approach toward the PRC than has been followed in recent years on issues ranging from most-favored-nation tariff treatment, Tibet, Hong Kong, Radio Free China, and Taiwan.

Meanwhile, the strong continuity in Chinese pragmatic behavior in world affairs has strengthened the arguments of those who push for a tougher U.S. policy in areas of U.S. disagreement with China. From this point of view, China has little alternative than to "go along" with U.S. pressure and accommodate to recent trends. Thus, rather than lose access to the U.S. market, China recently has accommodated on intellectual property rights issues and prison labor exports, accepted U.S. retaliation against illegitimate Chinese textile exports, and offered concessions in proliferation and human rights areas to help assure enough congressional support for continued MFN treatment by the United States. These Americans judge that the recent record shows that the United States can safely "jack up the pressure" concerning Chinese practices without serious risk that China will shift policies in ways adverse to U.S. interests. Some of this persuasion also argue that U.S. leverage is strong enough that the United States also can take other sensitive steps (for example, sales of advanced U.S. fighters to Taiwan; U.S.-backed political activities in Hong Kong; support for surrogate radio broadcasts to China) that in the past would have been deferred out of concern over a possible PRC reaction contrary to American interests. At bottom, these Americans judge that any significant Chinese action taken to retaliate against such U.S. pressures would likely do more damage to Chinese interests than to U.S. interests. Given the pragmatic record of recent Chinese policy, they judge that the likelihood of sharp change in Chinese policies is not great.

Even those Americans arguing for more moderation and engagement in U.S.-China policy generally agree that most Chinese options to retaliate against U.S. pressure would likely end up hurting China as much or more than the United States. They also tend to believe that the United States, as the political leader of developed countries, a major market for Chinese goods, the world's sole military superpower, and the leading influence in international political and financial organizations, exerts major long-term influence on China. President Bush underlined this point in a speech at Yale University in 1991.

But, these Americans add, the United States can easily mishandle its influence on China. Heavy-handed American pressure could cause China to cut off ties with the United States and attempt to pursue development without favorable access to the U.S. market or other advantage. This would clearly hurt China's growth and development, but Beijing leaders might judge that U.S. pressure had reached such sensitive levels that they had little choice than to accept the costs of a substantial downgrading with Washington. Beijing might judge that such actions would only have a short-term negative effect as Asian countries, including Japan, Taiwan, Hong Kong, and Korea, and probably also the European Community, would likely attempt to seek economic advantage from the U.S.-China downturn while privately pressing Washington to be more cautious in how it treats China for the sake of Asian and world stability. Under these circumstances, the United States could find that its leverage on China had been reduced as a result of its heavy pressure tactics. Washington's ability to promote change in China may be seen to require a prolonged engagement basically consistent with the policies of Japan and the EC that deepens China's interdependence with the developed world.

ENDNOTES

1. For up-to-date background and analysis on U.S.-China relations see CRS Issue Brief 92022. *China-U.S. Relations in the 1990s: Issues for Congress*, by Kerry Dumbaugh (updated regularly).

2. There are other dimensions to the debate that are not dealt with in this chapter. For example, some argue that China has become in recent years much less important to the United States, while others argue for China's continued importance for American concerns. Advocates of a moderate approach include a range of opinion on this question involving those who see China as important to the United States as well as those who judge that China's importance to American interests has declined substantially. At the same time, advocates of a tougher approach than followed in recent years include individuals with a similarly broad range of opinion on this question.

3. Among the many useful reviews of Chinese foreign policy and behavior in this period, see A. Doak Barnett, *China and the Major Powers in East Asia*, Brookings, 1977; Harry Harding (ed.), *China's Foreign Relations in the 1980s*, Yale, 1984; June Teufel Dreyer (ed.), *Chinese Defense and Foreign Policy*, Paragon House, 1989; Harry Harding, *A Fragile Relationship: The United States and China Since 1972*, Brookings, 1992; Samuel Kim (ed.), *China and the World*, Westview, 1989; Robert Sutter, *Chinese Foreign Policy: Developments After Mao*, Praeger, 1986; Yufan Hao and Guocang Huan (eds.), *The Chinese View of the World*, Pantheon, 1989; and Allen Whiting (ed.), "China's Foreign Relations," the *Annals*, January 1992.

4. This analysis draws heavily from Robert Sutter, *Chinese Foreign Policy in Asia and the Sino-Soviet Summit: Background,*

Prospects, and Implications for U.S. Policy, CRS Report 89-298 F, 15 May 1989, 7-11.

5. The political reforms fell notably short of political pluralism or democracy as there remained strong measures to prevent dissent from emerging as a serious challenge to the regime.

6. See review in Harding, *A Fragile Relationship,* op. cit., 173-214.

7. Among recent assessments of China's foreign policy behavior, see Whiting (ed.), *China's Foreign Relations,* op. cit.; *Current History,* September 1990, September 1991, and September 1992; Central Intelligence Agency, *The Chinese Economy in 1991 and 1992,* report prepared for the U.S. Congress, Joint Economic Committee, July 1992; and Atlantic Council-National Committee on U.S.-China Relations, "U.S.-China Relations at a Crossroads," draft, 1992.

8. In addition to sources cited above, see among others David Shambaugh, "China's Security Policy in the Post-Cold War Era, *Survival* (Summer 1992): 86-106; Michael Yahuda, "Chinese Foreign Policy and the Collapse of Communism," *SAIS Review* (Winter/Spring 1992): 125-37; and Nicholas Kristof, "As China Looks at World Order," *New York Times,* 21 April 1992, A1, A10. This and other sections also benefited from insights gleaned from interviews and consultations conducted with 20 U.S. Asian affairs specialists during July-September 1992.

9. Bonnie Glaser and Banning Garrett, Washington-based specialists who reviewed this project, were especially helpful in providing insights regarding the range and competing perspectives prevalent among foreign affairs specialists in China.

10. This view was especially prominent immediately after the successful U.S. war against Iraq in 1991. More recent Chinese views have a tendency to underline a trend toward

multipolarity rather than a unipolar world. (Interviews, Beijing and Shanghai, 1992; Washington, D.C., July-September 1992).

11. Interviews with PRC and U.S. officials, intellectuals, and other observers, Beijing and Shanghai, May 1992; Washington, July-September 1992.

12. There is debate among U.S. and other specialists as to why this seeming contradiction occurs and what it means for broader Chinese policy. Some see the PRC military bent on expansion and holding the upper hand in Chinese policy councils. Others judge that recent low-keyed warnings from the United States, Japan, ASEAN, and others should be enough incentive to get Chinese leaders to be less assertive in underlining China claims to disputed territory, and less likely to seek arms purchases that could be seen to seriously disrupt the balance of forces in Asia. (Interviews, September 1992).

13. Reviewed in CIA, *The Chinese Economy in 1991 and 1992*, op. cit.

14. See, among others, National Bureau of Asian Research, *The Future of China*, August 1992.

15. See articles by Steven Levine in *Annals*, January 1992, and Samuel Kim, *Current History*, September 1992.

16. See *Foreign Policy Debate in America*, CRS Report 91-833 by Robert Sutter and Charlotte Preece, 27 November 1991.

17. Recent events like the Bush administration's decision to sell 150 F-16 fighters to Taiwan and the administration's firm stance in negotiations over U.S. market access to China have made Chinese officials more uncertain as to what they can expect from the U.S. president, whether it be George Bush or Bill Clinton. Clinton in September 1992 identified himself with congressional critics of the Bush administration China policy (discussed at CRS seminar on China, 1 October 1992).

18. See, among others, the article by Allen Whiting in the *Annals, 1992* and the article by Samuel Kim in *Current History*, September 1992.

19. Some U.S. experts judge that there is a generational debate in China on Japan with younger Chinese specialists accepting Japan's playing a bigger role in world affairs.

20. See, among others, the article by Parris Chang in *Annals*, January 1992. See also CRS Report 92-658 S, *Taiwan-Mainland Relations—Implications for the United States*, by Robert Sutter, 6 August 1992, 26p.

21. For background, see article by Robert Ross in *Annals*, January 1992. See also CRS Report 92-118 F, *Indochina and Southeast Asia Under Change*, by Robert Sutter and Jeffrey Young, 31 January 1992, 19p.

22. See CRS Report 92-614 S, *East Asia: Disputed Islands and Offshore Claims—Issues for U.S. Policy*, by Robert Sutter, 28 July 1992, 15p.

23. Reviewed in articles by John Garver and Yitzhak Shichor in *Annals*, January 1992.

24. See, among others, *Chinese Missile and Nuclear Proliferation: Issues for Congress*, Shirley Kan, CRS Issue Brief 92056 (updated regularly).

25. This section benefited from discussions on this issue at a Center for Strategic and International Studies congressional breakfast, 9 June 1992, and a Woodrow Wilson Center seminar, 25 September 1992.

26. For background, see Harding, *A Fragile Relationship*, op. cit. This section benefited greatly from 20 interviews with U.S. specialists noted earlier and forums in China held in

Washington, D.C., in 1992 by the Asia Foundation, Woodrow Wilson Center, and CSIS.

27. Among questions raised in the discussion over how U.S. economic interests are served by China, there are the following:

- whether our bilateral trade balance with China is a meaningful index of our economic relationship;

- whether a flood of inexpensive imports from China is really a threat to American workers or whether it threatens the workers in other Asian economies (Hong Kong, Taiwan, South Korea, etc.) who previously produced comparable goods for export to the U.S. market;

- whether restrictions on Chinese imports are as likely to hurt American consumers (through higher prices) and American exporters (through Chinese retaliation) as to hurt the Chinese government;

- whether growing concern about Peking's long-term strategic intentions and military capabilities will create further debate on controls over the export of advanced technology to Peking.

CHAPTER SEVEN

Deng's China: What Lies Ahead?

ROBERT A. SCALAPINO

When the 14th Party Congress closed in Beijing on 18 October 1992 and the 1,989 delegates supposedly representing over 51 million CCP members began their journey home, Deng Xiaoping and his supporters could take great satisfaction in their handiwork.[1] The central theme of the Congress was "a socialist market economy," a phrase with precisely the amount of vagueness necessary for the times. The central pledge was that the accelerated reforms based on socialism with Chinese characteristics would continue for 100 years—surely time enough to get rid of all remaining Stalinist dinosaurs. Also, a slate of younger, better-educated technocrats replaced the remaining party elders in the Politburo and its all-important Standing Committee.

Politics were handled in a manner that signaled the hopes of the Dengists with respect to the next era. "Rightist tendencies" should continue to be fought, asserted Jiang Zemin, party secretary-general, in his speech before the Congress, and these centered upon negation of the Four Cardinal Principles: adhering to the socialist road, the people's democratic dictatorship, the leadership of the Chinese Communist party, and Marxism-Leninism-The Thought of Mao Zedong. In sum, "bourgeois liberalism" had to be fought and Leninism upheld on the political front so as to preserve stability. But the main threat, asserted Jiang, continued to come from "Leftist tendencies," a menace vividly illustrated during the 20 years after 1957. Such tendencies involved denying the correctness of the ongoing economic reforms, maintaining that those reforms

171

threatened a peaceful evolution to capitalism, and trying to distract attention from the central task of economic development by emphasizing the need for class struggle.[2]

Has pragmatism triumphed in China? Is the pattern of reform under the label of "socialism with Chinese characteristics" irreversible? What are the political consequences for China if economic development continues at an accelerated rate? While no certain answers to these basic questions are possible, I propose to advance some hypotheses about the present and future based upon the data now available.

First, one must assess the status of the Chinese economy after some 12 years of reform efforts. The positive side of the ledger is impressive. According to government figures, annual per capita income in cities and towns had reached 1,570 yuan in 1991, an increase of 3.9-fold over 1978, while peasant income totaled 710 yuan annually, a growth of 4.3 times over 1978.[3] These figures, moreover, do not take account of a second economy, unreported and very large. Improvements in food, clothing, and housing have been significant, especially for those in eastern China. Perhaps as many as one-half of the peasantry now have new or extensively renovated houses.

Private savings are massive, up to 1.4 trillion yuan in urban China alone.[4] GNP growth had averaged 7-8 percent per annum during the reform period, and the prospects were for a 10 percent growth in 1992. Increases in trade have been impressive, and foreign investment now totals some U.S. $30 billion, with a surge upward currently taking place.[5] China's total foreign debt at the end of 1990 was U.S. $52.5 billion, with a debt service ratio of 8.5 percent, well below the internationally recognized danger line.[6] Meanwhile, a structural shift in the economy has been underway. In 1981, the ratio of state-owned enterprises to total industrial output was 74.8; by 1991, it had dropped to 55 percent, with collectives accounting for 35 percent and private enterprise for 10 percent.[7]

Measured against the situation in other countries that previously followed a Stalinist economic strategy, China's economic picture is much brighter, perhaps partly because the reforms have been underway for more than a decade, but also because this society had an entrepreneurial spirit that could not be eliminated by 40 (but not 70) years of collectivism. While culture should not be over-emphasized at the expense of policy and other factors, neither should it be dismissed.

There is a more troubled side to the economic picture, however. In many respects, the Chinese economic reforms are in midstream, with many conflicting pressures brought to bear on the pace and thrust of future momentum. The commitment is to *both* the primacy of state ownership and the encouragement of a private sector. Yet the ills of the state sector are substantial and the remedies suggested have not yet worked. More than one-third of state-owned heavy and medium industries are operating at a deficit (some sources believe that the true figure might be as high as two-thirds), and the drain upon the national budget—which must cover that deficit—constitutes a major burden.

Prior to 1987, there was no incentive to make a profit, since losses were always covered, and given the artificial price structure, many plants had no chance to break even, let alone have a profit. After the 1987 reforms, a contract system between plant management and the state was inaugurated, with incentives established by allowing surplus profits over the contractual agreement to be used for new investments, welfare funds, and bonuses. In the absence of competitive markets and the influence of market forces, however, profits depend upon the bargain struck between management and the government, with that bargain subject to various irrational, highly personal factors. Moreover, in the absence of a social security system, the ability to rationalize the labor force is limited despite the permission given. Furthermore, with the state planning system currently in effect, these plants are still encouraged to meet quantity more than quality standards. Thus, huge inventories of unwanted, low-quality goods pile up in warehouses—but production goes on.[8]

Price reform is advancing, with an increasing number of products being bought and sold at market prices, but a two-tiered system still exists in certain vital areas, contributing to economic distortion. Once again, the current uneasy balance between market and state is revealed. Nor has the PRC found a way to avoid economic cycles of sizeable proportions. As 1992 comes to a close, the economy is again heating up, with industrial production running at least 18 percent above 1991. Throughout the country, every province and city seems determined to outdo its neighbor, and expansion of various types is massive. This not only makes for structural distortions and accentuates such bottlenecks as the energy shortage and a weak transport-communications infrastructure, it induces the threat of another round of excessive inflation. At the end of 1992, inflation in China's major cities was running close to 20 percent, although authorities insisted that for the country as a whole, it was only 5 percent.[9] Could another painful constriction such as that of 1988-89, which contributed mightily to the political unrest of that period, be avoided?

Another problem with strong political consequences looms large. Implicit in China's past and the nature of the current economic program, corruption is massive. With a significant number of officials having one foot in enterprises, public or private, and with access to the requirements for production often dependent upon personal "arrangements," favoritism and bribery of a wide range of types are near universal. This is powerfully abetted by the relatively low compensation for civil servants and party cadres.

Another group has suffered economically. Recent developments have turned China's intellectuals into a new branch of the proletariat. Especially those elements that are not in science-technology and cannot easily moonlight to augment their income are in serious straits. The implications of this for future development are acknowledged by the leadership, but little of a concrete nature has been done to improve the situation. On the contrary, punitive actions continue. China's two premier universities historically, Peking University and Fudan University in Shanghai, are still being punished for the Tiananmen incident by the requirement that their freshmen classes take one year of military training prior to entering classes, a policy that is affecting enrollments. Thus, a story now nearly a century old is continuing. Never since the end of the monarchical era has the Chinese government been able to come to terms with its intellectuals, whatever the lip service paid them and the needs of the modernization program.

Writ large, the central issues of the future in the economic realm are several. First, as the movement away from the old

174

centralized, planned economy continues, can the relationship between state and market evolve in a rational fashion, with the major contradictions eliminated or reduced? In all modern economies, there is an important role for the state in terms of macroeconomic policies that stimulate growth in directions suitable for the nation, given its resources and stage of development. Yet a heavy legacy of the recent past hangs over the Chinese economy, exemplified by the state-owned sector. An uneven mix between incentives and welfare continues. Further, state and market are interactive in a fashion that promotes corruption as it also retards economic rationality. Continued transformation is certain to be difficult, painful, and hotly contested by those who stand to lose—from blue-collar workers in possession of an iron rice bowl to managers who never worried in the past about profits or losses. Ultimately, the economic reforms aim at nothing less than a far-reaching change from the culture posited by Leninism. But whatever the trauma involved, it seems clear that the type of coexistence of state and market presently existing cannot endure for long, and traditional Chinese culture may be of some assistance in this respect.

Second, the process of decentralization—a concomitant of the reform program from the beginning—is irreversible. But what is the balance to be between national macroeconomic policies and subnational economic programs? At present, a strong element of provincial protectionism exists, reminiscent of the old liken taxes imposed by a province on transprovincial shipments in the early 20th century. Protectionism of various types is extensive at provincial levels. Further, uneconomic duplication of industrial plants is taking place. China does not need 700 television producers. Moreover, despite the great advantages of township industries in absorbing surplus rural labor and raising rural living standards, the extravagant use of raw materials and energy by such enterprises is a problem that must be faced sooner or later. Indeed, by the end of the century, the problem of energy along with that of inadequate transport and service industries will be heightened, even if major improvements in utilization are effected.

China must also absorb a new labor force of 15 to 17 million yearly between now and the end of the century. Already the

175

unemployed and underemployed peasantry constitute a pressure upon a number of the country's overpopulated cities despite the measures taken to keep the rural population in place.

One of the tasks of macroeconomic policies must be to stabilize demand and to channel the massive savings into investment to the extent possible. The need for technological modernization will steadily grow, and with it, the interdependence upon the advanced market economies. The determination to turn out must not lag, and that will require further measures to encourage foreign investment, including greater access to China's domestic market.

Finally, the massive bureaucracy that a combination of the command economy and omnipresent party has spawned must be trimmed and reoriented. Reportedly, as of 1991, China had 34 million individuals whose wages were included in governmental budgets at various levels, with that figure having grown from 15 million in 1979.[10] Thus, despite the reforms, the Chinese administrative structure is geared to an all-powerful, intrusive state and party operating a command economy. Can the pledge to tackle the deeply entrenched bureaucracy be implemented?

Despite the awesome challenges, there is reason for cautious optimism. The economic reforms and the goals now established for the coming years accord reasonably well with China's capabilities. The greatest uncertainties relate to how well the function of the state can be shaped so that it is a supporter of, rather than a competitor with, the private sector and how satisfactorily a balance between macroeconomic policies and regional-local initiatives can be achieved.

The determination of these matters is as much a political as an economic question. Thus, in the final analysis, one must fathom the future potentialities of Chinese politics. Two central political issues are now on the immediate horizon. One relates to the nature of future leadership. It is clear from a close examination of the current Politburo that China's top leaders are drawn predominately from what may be defined as the well-educated, technocratic class, closely tied to eastern China, and more particularly, key metropolitan areas, notably Shanghai.[11]

Of the seven Politburo Standing Committee members who stand at the pinnacle of the system, five can be placed in this general category. Only one (Li Ruihan) comes from a worker background, and only one (Liu Huaqing) has had a military career, with limited formal education except through military channels.

The same pattern generally holds with respect to other Politburo members. Seven have had advanced education and a technical-scientific background; only one comes from the "proletarian" class, with limited formal education, and similarly, only one has had a military career. While several have had Sichuan backgrounds, all have been in East China in recent years, with Shanghai (4), Beijing (3), Tianjin (1), Shandong (1) and the Northeast (2) represented.

This data suggests the nature of the effort that is underway to prepare for the post-Deng era in terms of leadership. The attempt is to create a collective leadership that relies heavily upon educated technocrats whose careers supposedly give them substantial influence in China's key industrial centers: Shanghai, Guangdong, and Tianjin, together with those who have been based in the capital of Beijing. By drawing in individuals of prestige from China's key eastern provinces and great metropolitan centers, with a nod to Sichuan, the most populous province, can a national fabric be constructed that will hold?

The answer to this question is heavily dependent upon the answer to a second question. Can China do without a paramount leader, an individual who symbolizes in a personal sense the summit of power and authority and who, indeed, may in fact exercise such power? If one surveys the history of modern China, since the Xinhai Revolution of 1911, a succession of such leaders emerged, with interludes of chaos: Yuan Shikai, Chiang Kai-shek, Mao Zedong, and finally Deng Xiaoping. In the recent 14th Party Congress, a giant paradox could be observed. Even as the framework of a collective leadership was being built, the cult of personality revolving around Deng was being elevated in a manner reminiscent of the Maoist era. In his report to the Congress, Jiang proclaimed Comrade Deng, the "core" of second-generation leadership, to be the chief architect of our socialist reform, of the open policy, of the modernization program, and an individual who respected the masses, paying "constant attention to the interests and aspirations of a majority of the people."[12] Having not yet recovered

177

from the cult of Mao, the current leaders seem to feel it is necessary to foster a cult of Deng in order to reach the masses, providing them with a new father.

The same approach is being used with respect to civil and military elites. Military cadets' education is to include less emphasis upon the Marxist classics and more time to be devoted to the study of Deng's thought. At various provincial party meetings, members are urged to reflect deeply upon Deng's writings. Suddenly, Deng's collected writings and pictures of the venerable elder statesman are to be found everywhere.

Mao's position has been stabilized insofar as the present party hierarchy is concerned. He should not be unduly criticized even though he made serious mistakes in the latter part of his career. He was the party "core" during the triumphal era when China stood up against imperialism and ended the long dark night of back-wardness. A great many ordinary Chinese may have gone further in rehabilitating Mao. He has been idolized quite literally, with his picture hung in car windows as crucifixes or other sacred symbols are displayed, to ward off danger. What part superstition, what part a longing for a father figure? In any case, the effort is to make Deng that figure today, with an emphasis on "his far-sighted vision of China's future."

In the light of the current campaign, a living Deng seems all the more crucial for the period immediately ahead. Can China be plunged into an uncertain era of rapid change without a supreme leader speaking with the authority of a sage? At one point, it seemed that Yang Shangkun could play a transitional role were he to survive Deng, but this now seems far less likely. The cult of Deng has become too intense, and Yang's role appears to be declining.

Will one of the third or fourth generation quickly assume the paramount position? The problem is that none of the individuals on the current horizon have the reach of Mao or Deng into all facets of power: party, government, and military. They are "specialists," with careers that placed their role primarily in one category. Indeed, the present titular leaders of party and government—Jiang Zemin and Li Peng—are regarded by knowledge-able Chinese as weak, products of the compromises worked out privately by China's *genro*. If leadership is a central issue for the future, a closely related and equally important issue is the allocation of authority among center, region, province, and locality. It should be immediately noted that this issue is vitally important for all continental-sized societies, irrespective of political system. Moreover, it is an issue never finally resolved, with the need for constant revisiting. Note the American experience where a civil war was fought over the issue in the 19th century, and in the 20th century, one president (Franklin Roosevelt) centralized authority in a decisive fashion and another (Ronald Reagan) decentralized authority extensively. Note also the fate of Russia where overly centralized authority combined with the unwillingness to undertake reforms in a timely fashion resulted in the collapse of the Soviet empire.

In China, the economic reform program has resulted in considerable political as well as economic decentralization despite the effort to keep Leninism largely intact in the political realm. The issue now is whether a balance can be struck. Decentralization is required for effective economic development and as a manifestation of the need for substantial autonomy if the country's major social and economic differences are to receive proper homage. But there is also a need to preserve a national structure that has sufficient coherence and power to pursue effective macro policies at home and to represent the Chinese people internationally. Can China find the proper balance between Beijing-centrism and quasi-anarchy?

The task may be made more difficult because of a new phenomena that is emerging rapidly throughout Asia, namely, the creation of new economic territories (NETs) that cut across political boundaries, combining resources, manpower, technology, and capital in compelling combinations.[13] Parts of China are being pulled into these NETs: Guangdong-Hong Kong-Taiwan, Fujian-Taiwan, Shandong-South Korea, and Southwest China-Southeast Asia among them. The issues of jurisdiction and political control raised by the development of NETs are far-reaching—but the thrust is to provide further impetus for decentralized political authority.

The decline of ideology in China as elsewhere would also appear to render the problem of national unity more complex.

179

When Marxism-Leninism reigned supreme, China's masses were given a common set of political values. How deeply these values penetrated and the extent to which they were personalized in a figure like Mao may be debated, but certainly the effort was to use ideology as a force binding all citizens together.

At present, Marxism-Leninism-The Thought of Mao Zedong is ritualistically emphasized on appropriate occasions such as the Party Congress, but the gap between rhetoric and reality grows steadily greater. Leaders stand by the new orthodoxy rhetorically—flexible, not rigid, MLM and socialism with Chinese characteristics. But policy at the highest levels as well as at lower echelons is dominated by the type of pragmatism symbolized some years ago by Deng's maxim, "It does not matter whether a cat is black or white, as long as it catches mice." Lenin—and even Mao—wherever they are, must surely be complaining to Marx.

In addition, the prestige of the party along with the government is at low ebb. One joins the party to enhance one's career, not out of idealism, as was the case among many individuals in the early days of Chinese communism. Cynicism and indifference are powerful forces in contemporary China, especially among younger generations. A number of Chinese of various ages are more interested at present in making money than in political involvement of any type.

To understand Chinese politics at present, an additional psychological-cultural dimension must be introduced. One aspect of Asian culture that China shares is the difference between one's outward expression and one's inner thoughts, or to put it differently, the distinction that should be drawn between statements and actions. This heritage is supremely important at a time when China's leaders must confront the need to make far-reaching policy changes without destroying the legitimacy of the revolution. Socialism based on MLM is to be staunchly upheld, but what Chinese leaders *do*, not what they *say*, defines MLM socialism at any given time.

As far as the masses are concerned, the decline of ideology places heightened premium upon the regime's performance. The new test is, "What have you done for me?," and often, with the word *lately* added. If the present PRC government is reasonably secure today, it is because rapid economic development is benefiting a sizeable number of the Chinese people, and they do not want to enter another period of instability like that which ensued during the Cultural Revolution.

Yet there is a gnawing anxiety among many of the top elite that economic success is sowing the seeds of future instability. Development in the economic realm is productive of three trends with important political implications: diversity, a growing "middle class," and greater conversance with the external world. Widening class differentiation together with radically different paces of sectoral and regional development challenge highly centralized, uniform policies. They make the emergence of multiple power centers inevitable. Further, the growth of a better-educated, economically comfortable urban "middle class" leads to demands for more genuine involvement in the political process. Moreover, a market-oriented economy together with the communications-information revolution brings greater interaction with other parts of the world, rendering isolation as a technique of control passé.

What is the answer? At present, the PRC leadership seeks to advance on two fronts. Economically, as noted, the themes are courage, determination, full steam ahead to accelerated development. Politically, the thrust is increasingly to stress nationalism, in part as a substitute for a comprehensive ideology. A renewed nationalist campaign of major proportions is underway in China. The positive focus is upon making China a great and powerful nation, respected by others. In addition, there is a defense of national sovereignty in classic 19th century terms. To be sure, this defense rests uneasily with the new currents of interdependence that are implicit in contemporary economic trends. Yet it is unequivocally set forth. The negative side of the nationalist message, and one with a historic appeal to Chinese, is "Do not allow foreigners to use 'peaceful evolution'—the new weapon in place of military intervention—to overthrow our system, interfering with our nation and denigrating our people as of old." It is a supreme irony that the remaining Leninist states including China—inheritors of such themes as the international brotherhood of the proletariat—are now making nationalism their supreme weapon in the effort to unify their people while the advanced industrial nations, classic defenders of nationalism, are being dragged, however reluctantly, toward internationalism. To be sure, the struggle between nationalism and internationalism is destined to be one of the epic battles of the coming decades throughout the world. But the remaining Leninists, having sought to skip capitalism and its supportive nationalist shield, now seek to return to these hallmarks of past Western progress.

Against this picture, what predictions may be ventured? On the economic front, it seems safe to assert that the commitment to a mixed economy, with a strong market quotient and an ever-larger degree of decentralization, is irreversible. The successes registered under the on-going experiment are too great, the negative lessons of the old command economy too powerful to permit otherwise.

What is more difficult to predict is whether the PRC government will be able to disentangle the state and private sector, especially in the industrial part of the economy, and reach a system that is economically rational. An increasing number of top officials appear willing to take the risks—and they are significant—of making the effort. But the current indications are that a combination of entrenched bureaucrats and disadvantaged workers will put up a strenuous battle. Thus, portions of the old order will constitute a drag on efficiency for the foreseeable future.

At the same time, an increasing portion of the economy will slip out from under the control of the government—central, provincial, or local. This is already well underway, and it cannot be prevented. As noted, a large second economy exists, fueled by "underground" official as well as private operations and combinations of them; this can only increase.

Growth rates will continue to be high, restricted mainly by the bottlenecks noted previously. But the economy will not escape the problem of cycles, some of them likely to be severe. In addition, regional differences will become more sizable despite efforts to curb them.

Under such conditions, China can only be held together by a strong government and one that can depend upon a supportive military. Fortunately for the leadership, the next generations of military leaders will almost certainly place their primary emphasis upon the modernization of the armed forces. Hence, they will need an expanding economy (one in which they participate directly) and a state that has maximum stability. As a result, they are likely to accept party leadership as long as the party can deliver on the economic front. Their interest in being directly involved in political leadership will be minimal *except* in border regions where security and political issues are closely intertwined. One may expect greater security-military power in such areas as Tibet, Xinjiang, and the northern frontier regions, as indeed, is the case today. In the final analysis, however, they are more likely to operate as a pressure group on government than to serve as the governors themselves. It should be noted, however, that the military has divisions on issues like reform that parallel those in the civilian sector, and no paramount military leader who can enforce unity may be a problem.

Taking all factors into consideration, the situation confronting China argues strongly against any early movement toward a multiparty system or the wide-ranging freedoms associated with a politically open society. The current emphasis on *stability and development* will remain the dominant theme. The current political scene harbors a paradox likely to continue for some time: China combines strong elements of a police state with a central government and party whose reach is declining. The leaders are cognizant of the need for political as well as economic reforms if appeals for support are to be effective. The call repeatedly goes out to purge corrupt cadres, to listen to the voice of the people, to be servants, not masters. A renewed emphasis, moreover, has been placed upon consulting "the democratic parties," those entities set up by the Communists supposedly to give voice to nonproletarian elements.

Further, it is clear that the perimeters of political permissibility have widened somewhat. Figures from the intellectual world publicly call for greater scope for the arts. Intellectuals discuss their economic problems openly, and while there is very limited freedom to write, the freedom to talk is considerable; there isn't the atmosphere of fear that pervaded the intellectual community during and immediately after the Cultural Revolution. In sum, the intellectual atmosphere is more fluid than is realized by many external observers.

This situation is unlikely to be reversed. Periodic crackdowns, directed mainly at individuals who cross over the obscurely drawn line, will take place. Nevertheless, the frontiers of permissibility will be constantly tested, and as old-guard cadres pass from the scene, and better educated, more technocratically inclined officials take the helm, the political lines will loosen. As noted earlier, however, a move to unrestricted political pluralism is more unlikely. The chances are strong that such a development under present conditions in China would quickly lead to chaos.

There is an alternate course, namely, what I have termed authoritarian-pluralism.[14] Under this system, politics is constrained, although not as tightly controlled as in the old Leninist system, with a single party (the CCP) dominant and multiple restrictions upon the freedoms that are required for a democratic society. But pluralism grows in the social sphere, with a civil society operating with increased autonomy from the state, and in the economy, the role of the market expands, although the state remains an important actor.

Meanwhile, control over China's minorities is certain to remain tight, along with efforts to satisfy some of their economic needs. There is no way in which cultures like that of the Tibetans or the Kazhak, Uighur, and Kyrgyz peoples of Xinjiang can be meshed with that of the Han. Even the Sinicization of Mongols and certain other minorities such as the Yi will continue to be difficult. Some degree of genuine autonomy for certain minorities would ease the current political strain, but that will not come easily as long as the military play a prominent role in the border regions, especially should unrest mount across those borders, as is entirely possible.

Minority unrest will not be regime-threatening because the combined minorities total only 8 percent of the Chinese population, and they are widely scattered geographically as well as being very diverse culturally. Nonetheless, ethnic minorities occupy more than 50 percent of China's total land area and serve as a reminder that China is an empire as well as a nation. They can cause problems, especially should they find support from external sources, and current Chinese leaders are acutely aware of this fact, hence, quick to quell any real or perceived dissidence.

In recent years, relieved of the burden of countering Russian political influence in Asia as well as Russian military power, China has significantly improved its diplomatic position in the region. With the emphasis upon accepting different political and social systems based on the Five Principles of Peaceful Coexistence, diplomatic relations have been established or reestablished with all six ASEAN states, with Vietnam, and with South as well as North Korea. Tension with India has been somewhat reduced, and relations with Russia as well as the Central Asian Republics have been normalized. Sino-Japanese relations have also improved. With Taiwan, unofficial and quasi-official ties have expanded. Only PRC-U.S. relations remain fraught with tensions and uncertainty.

Nonetheless, a close examination of these various relationships reveals an underlying fragility. China is huge, highly conscious of its perceived national interests, and generally self-confident, occasionally imperious, in dealing with the states around it. The recent nationalist surge, moreover, has underlined these traits. Understandably, neighboring states find it difficult to rest easily with the giant in their midst. Moreover, the overseas Chinese community in Southeast Asia has long evoked envy and suspicion on the part of indigenous populations.

Will the unresolved issues from the territorial to the economic be set aside or resolved peacefully through negotiations? That is the hope, and that is China's pledge. Nevertheless, a progressive modernization of China's military forces together with continued economic advances signal the possibility that China will be the preeminent regional power in East Asia at some point in the early 21st century. The other contender is Japan, but the obstacles to full-fledged Japanese economic, political, and military power in the region remain substantial. Russia may eventually regain its strength and role in Asia, but not in the near term. Uncertainties about the commitment of the United States will remain, despite American assurances. Hence, other Asian nations will treat China with a combination of respect and cooperation on the one hand, and caution together with apprehension on the other. Indeed, it is this ambivalence (which also marks the Japanese attitude) that powerfully underwrites the desire for a continuing American strategic as well as economic presence in Asia.

Yet if a powerful China evokes fear, a chaotic China would be equally troublesome, as most Asians realize. Should China disintegrate under the force of decentralization run rampant, a series of failures on the economic front, or a serious breakdown of unity among the political and military elites, the repercussions would spread far beyond China's borders, as they did in the earlier decades of this century. The prospects of conflict spilling over the borders, refugee flows, and a disruption of the economic integration now taking place are desired by no one.

While a negative scenario cannot be ruled out, it does not seem probable. Rather, China seems likely to remain viable as a political entity despite periodic crises and to score uneven economic advances in the years immediately ahead by combining political authoritarianism with social and economic pluralism. As noted earlier, however, Chinese politics will probably contain a rising element of pluralism under the veneer of the Leninist cover. The political system will constantly be tested as social and economic diversity expands and international contacts proliferate. The one certainty is that China will not remain static—the forces of change are too massive and too active to permit the status quo to be maintained.

ENDNOTES

1. The prelude to the 14th Party Congress and the events of the Congress itself were extensively covered in key PRC and Hong Kong newspapers and journals from the beginning of October. In English, one should consult the Foreign Broadcast Information Service, *Daily Report—China* for the same period, including four supplements specifically devoted to the Congress, *China Daily*, and *Beijing Review*.

2. Jiang's speech has been published in a number of sources. See, for example, *China Daily—Document Supplement*, 21 October 1992, 4.

3. *Renmin Ribao* (*People's Daily*), 14 October 1992, "Changes in Economic, Living Standards Viewed," carried in Beijing Xinhua in English, FBIS-CHI, 16 October 1992, 26–27.

4. This figure was given by Luo Gan, head of the cabinet secretariat, on 15 October 1992 and reported in Hong Kong AFP, reproduced in ibid., 16 October 1992, p. 17. Luo also reported that the rate of savings had increased most for private businessmen, actors, athletes, and other high-income professionals and that the total savings of ten million private businessmen exceeded the total savings of China's 800 million peasants. He expressed concern over growing class divisions and suggested that taxes on private incomes should be raised (p. 18). Labor Minister Ruan Chongwu indicated the same concern and supported more efficient tax collection.

5. These figures were given by Chicago Consul-General Wang Li in an address in St. Louis on 9 October 1992, published in Beijing *Zhongguo xinwen she* and reproduced in ibid., 16 October 1992, 3.

6. Kozue Hiraiwa, "Investment in China Gathering Momentum," JETRO, *China Newsletter*, May-June 1992, 1.

7. Ibid., 1.

8. For one analysis of this problem, see Zhai Linyu, "Current Situation and Problems of China's State Enterprises," *China Newsletter*, May-June 1992, 8-12.

9. See the news conference held by Li Lanqing, minister of foreign economic relations; Zhao Dongwan, minister of personnel; and Hong Hu, vice-minister of the State Commission for Restructuring the Economy, on 15 October, published in FBIS-CHI, 16 October 1992, 1-3. The acknowledgment in this conference regarding urban inflation was only that it was double-digit in certain cities.

10. "China to Carry Out Comprehensive Institutional Reform," Hong Kong *Liaowang Overseas Edition*, 21 September 1992, 3-4, as reproduced in FBIS-CHI, 14 October 1992, 17-20.

11. In its October 20 and 21 (1992) issues, *China Daily* presented a profile of each of the 20 Politburo members selected in the aftermath of the 14th Party Congress.

12. "Jiang Zemin's Report at Party Congress," *China Daily— Document Supplement*, op. cit., 2.

13. I sought to develop this theme in an article "The United States and Asia—Future Prospects," *Foreign Affairs*, Winter 1991/ 1992, 19–40.

14. See *The Politics of Development—Perspectives on 20th Century Asia*, Harvard University Press, 1989.

Editor and Contributor Information

A. DOAK BARNETT is Professor Emeritus and Head of the China Program at the Johns Hopkins School of Advanced International Affairs (SAIS) as well as Senior Fellow Emeritus at The Brookings Institution. Currently serving as a member of a State Department advisory panel on China and consultant to the National Security Council, he has written and edited more than 20 books and published numerous articles on China.

DEBORAH DAVIS is Professor of Sociology and Chair of the East Asian Program at Yale. She has been a visiting lecturer in Taiwan and Hong Kong. Among her recent books are *Chinese Families in the Post-Mao Era* and *Long Lives: Chinese Elderly and the Communist Revolution.*

JOHN FEI is Professor of Economics Emeritus at Yale University and President of Chung-hua Institute for Economic Research. A member of Academia Sinica, he has taught at Harvard and Cornell. His books include *Growth and Equity: The Taiwan Case* and *Transition of Open Dualist Economy.*

PAUL H. B. GODWIN is Associate Dean of Faculty and Academic Programs and Professor of National Security Policy at the National War College, Washington, D.C. He was a Visiting Professor at the Chinese People's Liberation Army National Defense University in Beijing, Fall 1987. His research and publication over the past 15 years has focused on Chinese security policy and defense modernization. His most recent publication is "Chinese Military Strategy Revised: Local and Limited War" in *The Annals of the American Academy of Political and Social Science*, Vol. 519 (January 1992).

189

JACK HOU is a Professor of Economics at California State University. A Ph.D. from Yale, he has his major publications in the field of Chinese economy.

SHAO-CHUAN LENG is Compton Professor of Government Emeritus and is currently in charge of the Asian leadership program at the Miller Center of Public Affairs, University of Virginia. Among his publications concerning the PRC are *Criminal Justice in Post-Mao China* and *Changes in China: Party, State, and Society.*

ROBERT SCALAPINO is Robson Professor of Government Emeritus at the University of California at Berkeley. Among his numerous publications are *Modern China and its Revolutionary Process* and *The Politics of Development: Perspectives on Twentieth-Century Asia.*

ROBERT SUTTER has specialized in Asian and Pacific affairs and U.S. foreign policy with the Congressional Research Service of the Library of Congress since 1977. He currently is Senior Specialist in International Policy with the Congressional Research Service and has published books and numerous articles dealing with contemporary China, Japan, Korea, and Indochina and their relations with the United States.

Index

DC- physicist. Norman Levine